THE KEEPERS OF COLOR

AND IF YOU SEARCH, YOU MIGHT DISCOVER
SOME REBELS WORKING UNDERCOVER
WHO ARE DETERMINED TO BE FREE.

JUST KNOW THE SAVIOR SAVES HIMSELF
IT CAN'T BE DONE BY SOMEONE ELSE
IT'S UP TO YOU, IT'S UP TO ME.
—Ben Lee, "Land of Criminals"

THE KEEPERS OF COLOR

A CREATIVE HERO'S JOURNEY INTO THE WORLD WITHIN

BY JON MARRO

WRITTEN AND ILLUSTRATED WITH YOU

ENLIVEN BOOKS

—

ATRIA

NEW YORK • LONDON • TORONTO • SYDNEY • NEW DELHI

An Imprint of Simon & Schuster, Inc.
1230 Avenue of the Americas
New York, NY 10020

First Enliven Books/Atria Paperback edition April 2018

This publication contains the opinions and ideas of its author. It is intended to provide helpful and informative material on the subjects addressed in the publication. It is sold with the understanding that the author and publisher are not engaged in rendering medical, health, or any other kind of personal professional services in the book. The reader should consult his or her medical, health, or other competent professional before adopting any of the suggestions in this book or drawing inferences from it.

The author and publisher specifically disclaim all responsibility for any liability, loss, or risk, personal or otherwise, that is incurred as a consequence, directly or indirectly, of the use and application of any of the contents of this book.

For information about special discounts for bulk purchases, please contact Simon & Schuster Special Sales at 1-866-506-1949 or business@simonandschuster.com.

The Simon & Schuster Speakers Bureau can bring authors to your live event. For more information or to book an event, contact the Simon & Schuster Speakers Bureau at 1-866-248-3049 or visit our website at www.simonspeakers.com.

Manufactured in China

10 9 8 7 6 5 4 3 2 1

Library of Congress Cataloging-in-Publication Data
Names: Marro, Jon, author.
Title: The keepers of color : a creative hero's journey into the playful paradox called life / Jon Marro.
Description: First Atria paperback edition. | New York : Enliven Books, 2018.
Identifiers: LCCN 2017032349 (print) | LCCN 2017045060 (ebook) | ISBN 9781501167683 (eBook) | ISBN 9781501167676 (pbk)
Subjects: LCSH: Spiritual biography—Miscellanea. | Spirituality—Miscellanea. | Coloring books.
Classification: LCC BL71.5 (ebook) | LCC BL71.5 .M37 2018 (print) | DDC 204—dc23
LC record available at https://lccn.loc.gov/2017032349

ISBN 978-1-5011-6767-6
ISBN 978-1-5011-6768-3 (ebook)

If you bring forth what is within you, what you bring forth will save you.
If you do not bring forth what is within you,
what you do not bring forth will destroy you.
—Gospel of Thomas

◆ IN DEDICATION ◆

To **Susan Waters-Eller**, an artist, teacher, mentor, visionary, and friend who first introduced me to the quote above and who through decades of guidance, conversation, and critique has never once spoken to "me" but rather always to the artist who lives within me—and in so doing gave me the creative cartography that made this book possible.

To **Matthew and Terces Engelhart** for your Eternal Presence, for being the headwaters of the Abounding River, and for nourishing me countless times through the medicine of food, the wisdom of love, and the prayer of Gratitude.

And to **Ciela**, because she knows what is within me, she Sparcs it to life, and she's my hero.

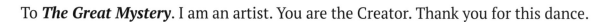

THANKS BE TO YOU

To **The Great Mystery**. I am an artist. You are the Creator. Thank you for this dance.

Tiffany Kolchins, for being my sure-footed Sherpa and taking this journey with me. For being there (even when we didn't know where "there" was) every step of the way. You were the earth under my feet, the fire under my seat, the light up ahead, and the "do this instead." This book simply would not be without you. And a special thank-you to **Caitlin Kolchins** for your brave and adventurous spirit, so wise and willing beyond your years, and for being this book's first-ever *Keeper of Color*.

Zhena Muzyka, for believing with every imaginal cell in your being that everyone has a story to tell. For knowing that there were two stories within me: the one I wanted to write and the one that wanted to be written through me. And for empowering me with the tools, the trust, and the time to allow the latter to come through so brilliantly. You *Enliven* the world.

To my **Simon & Schuster** All-Stars: **Dana Sloan,** for how you lay out any problem and design its solution with such a caring calmness. **Ben Holmes,** for your patience while editing each pass of this book as if it were uniquely precious. **Haley Weaver,** for being so wonderfully professional, clearheaded, and on top of everything while I made many a creative mess. Thank you all.

Alyssa Reuben and Katelyn Dougherty at **Paradigm,** for being the dots in my i's and the crosses in my t's. This book is bound by your care and conduct, and you two are my change *agents*.

Mom and Dad, for being my first storytellers, and **Matt and Than,** for being the first ones I wanted to share them with.

Jason, Christina, and Big Girl Mraz, for teaching me that public can be private, modest is magnanimous, and simple is so spectacular. Thanks to you and the land for allowing me to give birth to myself, feeding me as I did so, and holding space for thirteen years to witness Plan B become Plan A.

Ryan Dilmore, for buying tickets early to see the midnight screening of anything I make, even though you already have an all-access pass and you're in the band.

Blair Wojcik, for your love of words and knowledge of good verses evil. You edited this book into what it is today, and in so doing left it WAY more beautiful than you found it.

James Kirkland, for your love of storytelling and for always picking up the phone.

Jenn Lutzenberger-Phillips, for constantly bringing something never-been-done-before into the world. For your love of systems and pyschology. And for being Color's grammar teacher.

Eva Ackerman and Land of the Lovely, for how you create ceremony in song and the sacred in spaces.

Lydia Hoffman, for being a kindergartener for life, a teacher of teachers, and a liver of purpose.

Justin, Rachel, and Arthur Padfoot Jonte, for being forever family and the neighboring certified organic soil that this *Seed of Hope* was planted in. Viva La Paloma!

Richard Condon, for your warrior's willingness to continuously dive *"once more unto the breach, dear friend"*; and all the *LEAPsters* for calling forth my calling.

Ryland and Sarah Engelhart, for your love, support, and the infinite ways you *Kiss the Ground*.

Josh Radnor, for being part Dios, part Man, and all brother who believes in me; for your open-door Dioshouse policy; and for the guiding light with which you write, inspiring me to color with words.

Trent Knott, this book is inspired by the one I know you'll write.

Melissa Sujata Smith, Mike Sherbakov, Pink Ninja, and the Mantra Yoga Community: Namaste.

Joseph Jacques, for living heroically from conception to cremation. You are a harmonic human.

Billy Galewood, for being a living permission slip to reinvent myself and let expression lead the way.

Ben Lee, for writing myths into melodies. This book is my "learning to love in the *Land of Criminals*."

Adrienne Fodor, for always sending me pictures, seeing the big picture, and then cheering me on as I color it in.

Robert James Ryan III, for your deep, inquiring heart and for encouraging me to roar.

Hannah Marro, for your cousinly support and for helping me chart the course to right where I belong.

Irene Tsouprake, for knowing your truth and being the loving wings so many others find theirs within.

Peter Harding, for our brotherhood and for how we lovingly push each other to be our best.

Stephanie Gonzalez and Light of Mine, for being the flickering flame of a life lived lit.

Mike George, for making sure this book lived, spoke, and Colored from its calling.

Andrew Dawson, for your genius for synthesizing giant ideas into simply stated ones.

Calie, **Kevin, and Aya Bohm,** for being medicinally intuitive triathletes in laughter, love, and Scrunch.

Suzi Prentiss, for your patient perspective and courageous compassion, and for being my *Mother Nurture*.

Craig Phillips and SunnyBoy, for teaching Color how to walk; and **Mike Gibson,** for knowing he can fly.

To each and every **Joan of Sparc,** for *bringing your Inner World to Life*.

Evryman, for always stoking the campfire and for the check-ins. This book was my rite of passage. Aho!

Joseph Campbell, Julia Cameron, Stephen Cope, Jack Kornfield, Richard Rohr, Carol S. Pearson, Michael Meade, Alana Fairchild, Omraam Mikhaël Aïvanhov, Marilyn Ferguson, Steven Pressfield, Clarissa Pinkola Estes, Lao Tzu, Carl Jung, Trevor Hall, Buddha, and Jesus—you were each my guide.

Shekhinah Mountainwater, for the use of "We Are the Flow" lyrics (facebook.com/ShekhinahFanPage); and **Michael Gelb,** for teaching me *How to Think Like Leonardo da Vinci* (michaelgelb.com).

To the mysticism, mythology, and symbolism within all spiritual traditions—you inspire my paints, pencils, and artistic utensils. Thank you for lighting the way.

To my friends, family, and teachers, past and present—your love has shaped me and thus this book.

To anyone who's ever put pen to paper, hands to prayer, or one foot in front of the other when all seemed lost and believing in yourself was the only way forward: You've got this.

◈ ABOUT THIS BOOK ◈

Inspired by Joseph Campbell and his lifelong study of the Hero's Journey, *The Keepers of Color* is designed to take you on an adventure into yourself. Its aim is to reawaken your sense of wonder, imagination, and boundless creativity as you move from your fears and doubts into your hopes and dreams.

This is you:

YOU ARE HERE:

YOUR GOAL IS TO GET HERE:

  Along the way, you will meet a trusty guide named *Color*. When you encounter *Color*, you'll be greeted with check-ins, emotional support, and inspirational cheerleading. *Color* is here to guide you through the uncharted territory within you.

You'll also encounter some *Keepers*, who are archetypal allies offering tales and talismans to support you through the book. *The Keepers* will present personal inquiries, creative tasks, and rewards for completing those tasks. There are twelve *Keepers* in total, with a few additional activities to explore and uncover. A suggested pace would be to complete one page per day or one to three *Keepers* per week.

Now, a few things you should know about *The Keepers*:

1.) They are on your team. They want what's best for you. They want your brightest, most blessedly beautiful life imaginable.

2.) They are going to ask you some questions, known as *Within-quiries*. These can be tough questions that may seem difficult to answer or put into words. Try to answer them honestly, openly, and as best you can.

Lastly, this book contains a Myth, which is a story that binds the *Keepers*' world to yours. Myths are like dreams, holding universal concepts that help tribes, cultures, and communities navigate from the mundane to the mystical.
This particular Myth is intended to empower you to tell your own story.

From the Artist & Author:
The Keepers of Color is part coloring book, part journal, and part folk tale sparked by the wild and uncertain times we're living in. It will ask you to contemplate the very simple but very profound question of why *you are here.*

The book's genuine intention is to remind you of the life you are capable of living. Consider it a training ground where you can creatively conquer your resistances and practice playing full-out by giving your whole heart to something. If you go too slow, you may lose momentum, and if you go too fast, you may lose the lessons. So pace yourself, push yourself, and remember to *be* yourself. Onward & Inward!

JON MARRO♡

SOME COLORFUL LANGUAGE

The Great Mystery: Often referred to by many names, including God, Creator, Spirit, the Universe, Allah, etc., *The Great Mystery* is this book's term for the Source of Life and all existence.

The World as We Know It: Generally speaking, this refers to the reality we experience through living a life on Earth.

The World Within: The inner realm, often described as "the Soul." This is the place where imagination and hope reside, where dreams and intuition come alive and emotions and feelings flow freely.

The Seed of Hope: The kernel and incandescent spark that holds your unique dreams and prayers. *The Seed* is buried deep inside *The World Within* and is your life in potential.

The Tree of Transformation: *The Tree* is a beacon of faith. Its roots are firmly planted in *The World Within*, while its branches and fruits spread out into *The World as We Know It*. *The Tree* is your fullest life realized and what *The Seed of Hope* grows into through your nature and nurture.

The Rainbow of Remembrance: A full-circle rainbow that spans like a bridge from *The World Within* to *The World as We Know It*. When *The World Within* is healthy, *The Rainbow* is vibrant and bright. When you forget to continually explore *The World Within* or wander off your path in *The World as We Know It*, *The Rainbow* starts to fade, and both worlds lose color and light.

The Keepers of Color: A group of guardians each assigned to protect and preside over a color in the spectrum. Each time you meet a *Keeper*, color him or her in, and fulfill his or her tasks, you reinvigorate *The Rainbow* and brighten *The World Within*.

Keepsakes: As you complete the activities and tasks asked of you, each *Keeper* will grant you a *Keepsake*. This is a unique talisman that symbolizes the lessons you have learned; it's a magical artifact for you to take on your journey through this book and beyond!

The Gray Area: A strange, foggy, cloud-like state of ambiguity and confusion. It is the enemy and adversary in this book, inflicting doubt and disarray on *The Keepers* and readers.

Color: *Color* (the character) is the spritely Sherpa and well-intentioned guide on your journey. *Color* (the spectrum) is a vibrant palette of expression that you can harness to bring your dream to life.

This is a tale that reminds other tales it is their time to be told.

Once inside a time *The World Within* was full of color and light. Imagination and creativity were the laws and loves of the land, held in balance from all directions by *The Great Mystery*. *The Great Mystery* has a million names, all of which point to the loving, luminous Source of Life that dwells inside every atom in every thing. It is the benevolent force that pumps blood through our body, guides rivers to the ocean, spins the planets in orbit, and turns winters to springs.

Stretching from one corner of *The World Within* to the farthest reaches of *The World as We Know It* spanned *The Rainbow of Remembrance*. *The Rainbow* was a brilliant and beautiful bridge that connected the heavens to the earth and the eternal to the present. It was a resplendent reminder of the magic that could be found not in some faraway land or on some enlightened mountaintop but here and now in this breathtakingly majestic world.

All creatures who dwelled beneath this colorful curve believed in the power of possibility. It was a place where dreams mattered, and every being was guided along their one-of-a-kind journey to live out a uniquely magnificent purpose.

To ensure that *The Rainbow of Remembrance* shone morning, noon, and night, the wisest of sages throughout this kingdom were employed to safeguard the spectrum. Each was assigned a hue in *The Rainbow*, conveyed a virtue to live by, and offered a talisman for the taking. Collectively, these kind and courageous custodians were called *The Keepers of Color*. *The Keepers* were a festive, celebratory bunch entrusted to color in everything under the sun. From bird wings to coral reefs, the nuances of Nature were all painted in praise and play. Wherever there was Color, there was Life.

But as is true with guardians of anything sacred, *The Keepers of Color* would all soon be tested.

One day, and no one knew quite how or why, and though many denied it or looked the other way, it started to happen. Dreams began disappearing. Like a thief in the night, something invisible and unseen snuck in, and soon *The World Within* became subdued, covered in a hazy, nebulous fog of forgetfulness. *The World* was in a crisis of Color.

A mysterious shadow formed like a sedating mist atop the land. It tore apart families, estranged neighbors, and isolated nations. Distraction and devastation ran free, while chaos and suffering grew into merciless tyrants. Something needed to change, but *something* was unwilling to.

Thankfully, even amid the surrounding gloom, there was a glimmer— a small yet immensely powerful *Seed of Hope*. Within this seed, the destiny of *The World* and the promise of its soul rested.

The Keepers sent out calls for help across all the kingdoms, hoping that someone, *anyone*, would answer. Their calls beckoned to those who would break out of their protective shells of comfort and conformity, inviting each being to sprout toward a new life and push beyond the all-encompassing darkness into the light of another reality. Little did they know that help would arrive from the most reluctant and unsuspecting of heroes . . .

I've been meaning to talk to you.
I made SUCH an embarrassing mistake.
You *promise* you won't be mad?
Okay. Here goes . . .

It's my job to watch over your dream so it doesn't wander or fly away.

But I got distracted.

Caught up in the busy–ness and the drama of the life you weren't really living. And when I turned around,

IT WAS GONE.

So, now I need your help to get it back.

I'm an inhabitant of your heart—your dream's reminder-in-residence. When you're living your purpose, I'm living mine, too. So it's important to both of us that you find your dream.

The good news is: *It's still inside you.*

(Somewhere.)

The even better news is:
We get to go on an adventure to find it!

Don't worry, we can pack light: all you'll need are some crayons, colored pencils, and/or markers —the more colors the better!

There's just one last little teensy condition. I promise this is it, and then we'll literally be on the same page.

You will need to say **YES** to the adventure.

You don't have to, of course—it is *your* life, after all, but I'm going after your dream, and if you want to come with me, all you have to do is turn the next page.

If not, no problem. You can put this book down or simply sit and stare at that *mysterious ladder that leads to everything you've ever hoped for or envisioned deep within yourself.*

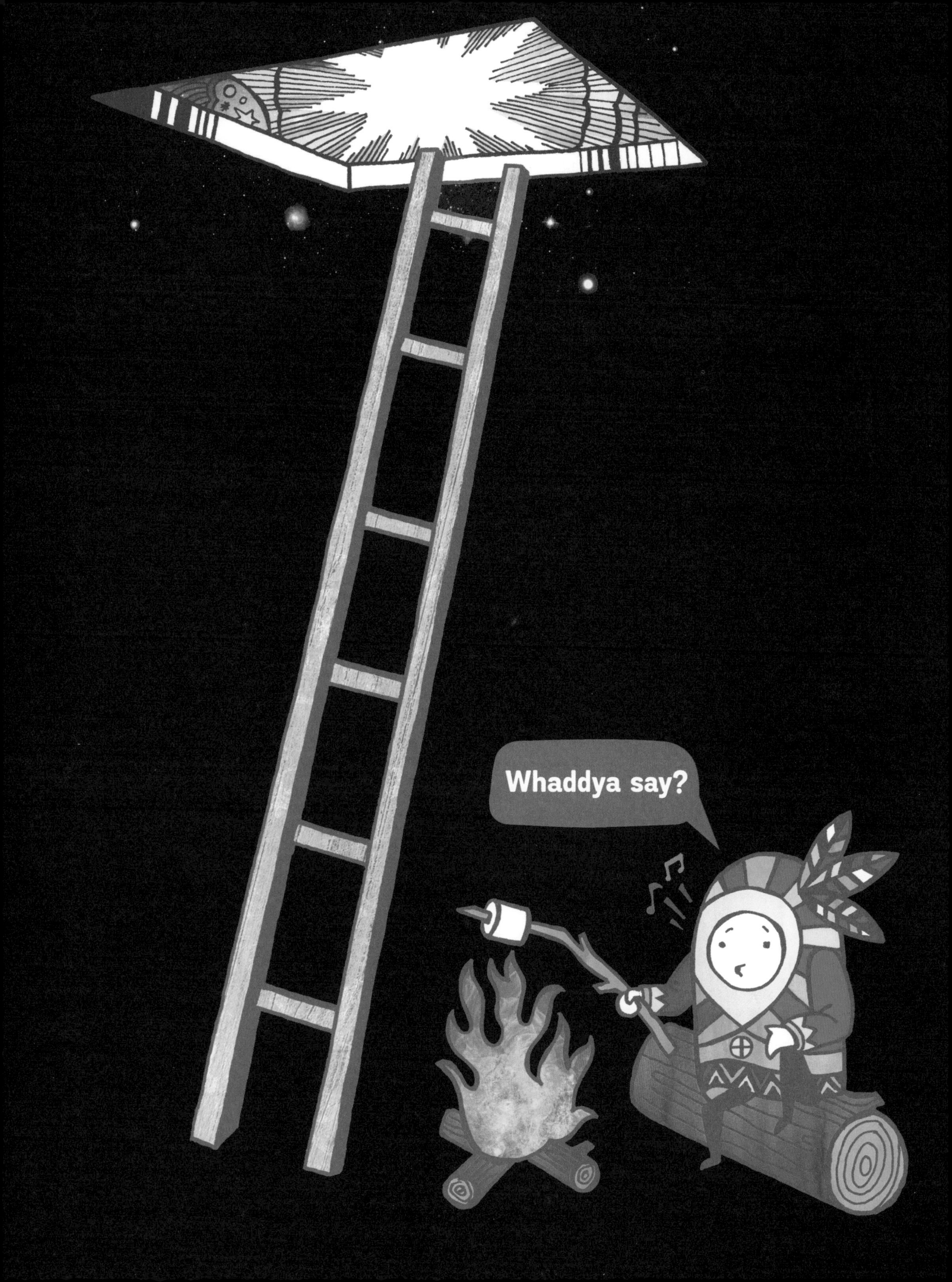
Whaddya say?

LIVING IN DECISION

Making a decision takes a moment.
Living a decision takes a lifetime.
—Sherif A. El-Mawardy

HI, DIVE.

Okay! Here we are, right where we want to be, on the edge of discovery. The adventure begins in the waters below.

Get your coloring utensil in hand! We're gonna jump right in!

On the next page, draw a waterline to determine how high we must jump and how deep we will dive. You literally have to draw the line somewhere. Don't worry—you cannot do this incorrectly.

To dive, put your hands in the prayer position. Point them toward the adventure below and let them lead you in. As a bonus exercise, you can draw and color in what lies swimming in the waters of your soul. Are there Whales of Worry? Eels of Envy? Some Seaweed of Shame? Just so you know, I'll keep everything in this book between us. Below are what I call "Within-quiries." These are important questions that, once answered honestly, help us discover clues to find your dream!

❖ WITHIN-QUIRIES: ❖

Where in life do you stop yourself from going "all in"?

....
....
....

What compelled you to say YES to this adventure?

....
....
....

The Edge . . . there is no honest way to explain it, because the only people
who really know where it is are the ones who have gone over.
—Hunter S. Thompson

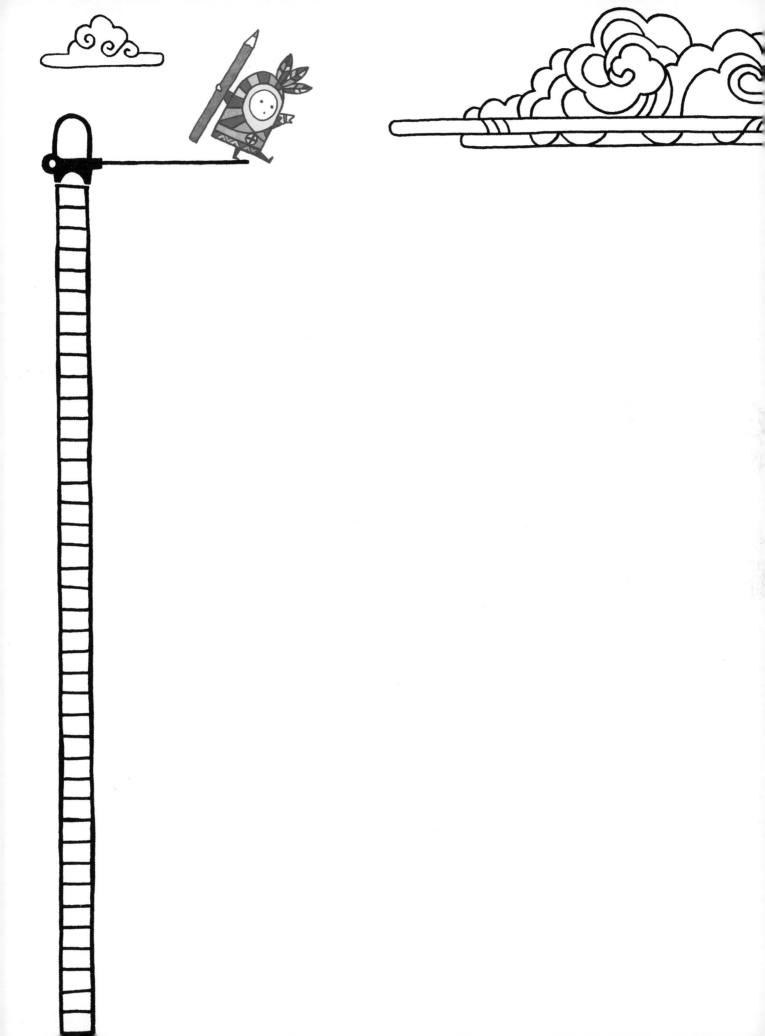

A SPLASH OF COLOR

Pearls don't lie on the seashore.
If you want one, you must dive for it.
—Chinese proverb

WET YOUR PALETTE

Not everyone tastes the waters of their own adventure. Now that we've entered this brave new world, let's make a splash! I see some hidden friends and treasures splattered among the seascape on the next page! Let's color in this wavy world and swim in the satisfaction of having leapt!

◆❖ WITHIN-QUIRIES: ❖◆

List three times you dove in heart-first.

1. ....
2. ....
3. ....

What does it feel like to be fully immersed in what you love?

....
....
....
....
....

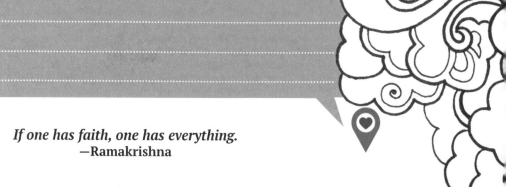

If one has faith, one has everything.
—Ramakrishna

Wow.
You did it. You leapt!
We crossed the
threshold of a whole new
realm of possibility.

(Possibly.)

Thankfully, so many
others have come before and
left some signposts along the
way, just like this one. This is
actually our map. If you follow
the map, you'll always come
right back to where you are—
except you'll be different.

YOU
ARE
HERE

You'll have
gone on a
journey!

You'll learn some things.
Let go of some things.
Sometimes you'll know
what to do, and
sometimes you won't.

It'll be just like life, and
I promise you'll be fine.

(I mean, most likely you'll
be fine. Because what's an
adventure without a
little danger?)

Don't worry: you won't be alone. I'll keep close, your guide-on-the-side. And we've got help: I know this team on the inside. They're called ***THE KEEPERS OF COLOR.***

(Gahhh, I'm freaking out! They're totally a big deal!)

The Keepers have a vested interest in you. They become more alive the brighter your *World Within* becomes. And nothing brightens *The World Within* more than a dream!

Oh—I almost forgot to mention that we're in search of a seed! Right now, your dream is being protected in a magical little kernel of belief called *The Seed of Hope.*

Have you ever felt it? That little wiggle as it's tried to take root? To find a seed, you have to think like a seed and act like a seed. You're going to have to commit to growing, unfurling, and breaking out of your shell, to stretching and reaching for the new life that's calling. *The Keepers* and I are here to invite you to take action in your life and create the most nourishing soil in which your *Seed* can grow.

HEARING THE CALL

There is a voice that doesn't use words. Listen.
—Rumi

When we begin to truly listen, new worlds open within us, and it is not unsurprising that we begin to hear a whole lot more. Oftentimes, that "more" comes in the form of more static, more noise, and more calls to endless adventures. It can be hard to know who's who and just how and when to listen.

Thankfully, the soul is a loyal and loving companion and always finds new messengers to dispatch the summonses requesting our attention. Sometimes these messengers come in the form of life lessons or wise words from a friend, and sometimes they appear in the form of a dolphin dressed in an indigenous sea-vest. Meet *Oído*, a porpoise with a purpose and *Keeper of the Color Blue*.

Oído was born in the silence of the depths. His mother was the ocean. His father was the very first sound ever made—a deep, melodious, primordial sound—the sacred syllable "Om." Om is believed to be the sound of creation, and thus the first-ever call to adventure. Oído was literally born to fulfill his calling.

Oído knows that no matter how much chaos and confusion there appear to be, somewhere deep inside, *The Seed of Hope* is quietly waiting and whispering the perfect instructions out of any mess we may find ourselves in.
Learning how to listen is learning how to Be. Hear. Now.

I AM MY COLOR'S KEEPER
NAME: OÍDO (OH-WEE-DO)
ANIMAL TOTEM: PORPOISE WITH A PURPOSE
KEEPER OF THE COLOR: BLUE
VIRTUE: LISTENING TO THE HEART
AFFIRMATION:
I TRUST MY INNER GUIDANCE
KEEPSAKE: CONCH

Color in Oído and lend him your ear so he can guide you in learning the simple and sage advice of listening to your own heart.

Let us be silent, that we may hear the whisper of God.
—Ralph Waldo Emerson

OÍDO

PUT THE COMPASS IN COMPASSION

If a man knows not to which port he sails, no wind is favorable.
—Lucius Annacus Seneca

DREAMCATCHER EXERCISE: MORALE COMPASS

Not everybody knows what their dream is or can hear their calling clearly. Sometimes in a world overflowing with options it can be hard to know exactly what you want. And even when we *know* how we feel, it can still be tricky to know how to navigate something as fleeting as an emotion or a desire. Our calling typically runs deeper. It serves something larger than ourselves. In fact, if your dream is only self-serving, consider that it may not be your true calling. Your calling begins with you but is not about you. Make sense? To help you find your True North, think of a moment in your life that touched your heart or a time when you were completely lit up. What about that moment moved you? What was your inner compass pointing to? On the right-hand page, color in the compass so it can chart the way to discovering the wonders inside you.

❖ WITHIN-QUIRIES: ❖

Where have you lost your way?

Where is your intuition currently guiding you?

Go confidently in the direction of your dreams! Live the life you've imagined.
—Henry David Thoreau

MADE IN VOYAGE

Sometimes God calms the storm. Sometimes he calms the sailor.
—Anonymous

LEADER SHIP

As we embark on the adventure to follow a dream or an inner calling, it can seem unsettling, like we are in a very small boat in the middle of the wide-open ocean—at night! A voyage beyond *The World as We Know It* and a search for something deeper than it offers, the making of this "night-sea journey" is an important rite of passage in any dream-catching.

On our crusade into the unknown there surely will be *Sirens of Seduction*, *Whirlpools of Worry*, and *Tentacles of Temptation*, but we must remember: no matter how choppy the waters may seem, we are also always aided by unseen forces that constantly keep the wind in our sails.

On the following page, decorate and color our ship and the ocean waves that will carry us to the other shores. Fill our ship with reminders of inspiration, hope, and cheer. Draw a meaningful image, icon, herald, or crest to be proudly embroidered on our ship's sail! Write the ship's motto on the side of the hull to remind our crew of when all seems lost. Bravery is our buoyancy and trust is our trade wind, so let's set sail to reunite with the dawning of our dream!

What are your three biggest distractions?

1. ....
2. ....
3. ....

What hopeful horizon are you finally ready to chart a course for?

....
....
....
....

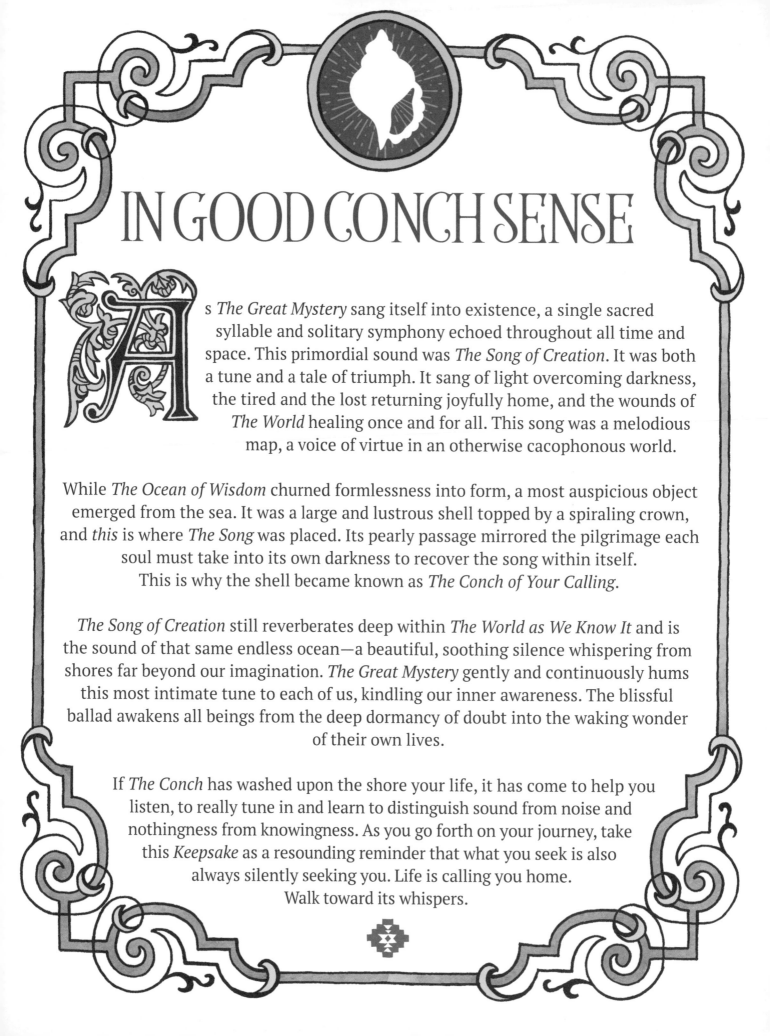

IN GOOD CONCH SENSE

As *The Great Mystery* sang itself into existence, a single sacred syllable and solitary symphony echoed throughout all time and space. This primordial sound was *The Song of Creation*. It was both a tune and a tale of triumph. It sang of light overcoming darkness, the tired and the lost returning joyfully home, and the wounds of *The World* healing once and for all. This song was a melodious map, a voice of virtue in an otherwise cacophonous world.

While *The Ocean of Wisdom* churned formlessness into form, a most auspicious object emerged from the sea. It was a large and lustrous shell topped by a spiraling crown, and *this* is where *The Song* was placed. Its pearly passage mirrored the pilgrimage each soul must take into its own darkness to recover the song within itself. This is why the shell became known as *The Conch of Your Calling*.

The Song of Creation still reverberates deep within *The World as We Know It* and is the sound of that same endless ocean—a beautiful, soothing silence whispering from shores far beyond our imagination. *The Great Mystery* gently and continuously hums this most intimate tune to each of us, kindling our inner awareness. The blissful ballad awakens all beings from the deep dormancy of doubt into the waking wonder of their own lives.

If *The Conch* has washed upon the shore your life, it has come to help you listen, to really tune in and learn to distinguish sound from noise and nothingness from knowingness. As you go forth on your journey, take this *Keepsake* as a resounding reminder that what you seek is also always silently seeking you. Life is calling you home. Walk toward its whispers.

THE CONCH OF YOUR CALLING

THE ROADLESS TRAVEL

The only person you are destined to become is the person you decide to be.
—Ralph Waldo Emerson

Beyond what we can see with the naked eye, and whether we believe it or not, islands, like people, are always connected beneath the surface. Born at the bottom of the sea, *Tuga*, *the Turtle of Tolerance*, longed to taste the faraway world called "Air." It took ten billion years, but patiently he swam, and one day he found the ceiling of the sea. As he rose to the surface and took his very first breath, Tuga and his shell became "Land." And though it took another ten billion years, life was breathed onto the Earth.

Tuga is the only one old enough to remember *The Creation of Things*. He has seen all things come and go, made Eternity his ally, and allowed *The Seed of Hope* to grow on its own time. Tuga trusts that there is always Life below the surface and that it emerges at the perfect moment, aided by *The Great Mystery*.

Tuga keeps his eyes on the prize, his feet on the earth, and his heart toward the heavens. Home is where his heart is, and while the world may be spinning in a sprint toward deadlines, bottom lines, and finish lines, Tuga keeps on *Keepering* on, knowing in the depths of his shell the wise words of Lao Tzu, who said: "Nature does not hurry, yet everything is accomplished." Enjoy becoming fast friends with a slowpoke and *Keeper of the Color Green*.

I AM MY COLOR'S KEEPER

NAME: TUGA (TOO-GA)
ANIMAL TOTEM: TURTLE OF TOLERANCE
KEEPER OF THE COLOR: GREEN
VIRTUE: TRUSTING THE PROCESS
AFFIRMATION:
MY LIFE UNFOLDS IN PERFECT TIMING
KEEPSAKE: KEY

Take your time coloring in Tuga and completing all his turtley tasks.

Make haste slowly.
—Augustus Ceasar

TUGA

UP, UPEND A WAY

Wisely, and slow. They stumble that run fast.
—William Shakspeare

OVERTURNED TURTLES

Look to the areas in your life where something is not sitting right. These could be debts or bills you have to pay, conversations you know you need to have, appointments you need to make, or chores you have been avoiding. These items left untended to can create roadblocks and detours on the path toward your dream. On the next page, name three places in your life calling for your attention, and write the action steps required to get things back on track. Color in the turtles and then color in your calendar on the date when you will set things straight.

Remember: the fulfillment of your purpose is something that is built slowly, over time, with simple, everyday steps.

❖ WITHIN-QUIRIES: ❖

Describe your biggest failure.

How has patience paid off in your life?

The journey starts with a single step—not with thinking about taking a step.
—Jeff Olson

THE ART OF ATTENTION

Adopt the pace of Nature: her secret is patience.
—Ralph Waldo Emerson

HEAVEN & SHELL

When you're living your purpose, time feels like it no longer exists. As you begin to look for your calling or start realizing your dream, something you may notice is how you travel and flow through time. Remember, patience is powerful, so take your time as you begin to color in this mandala. Carefully choose each color and its placement, and enjoy the gift of relaxation and the rewards that focus and attention bring. The divine is in the details. Look to your own life and see if there is an activity, hobby, or practice you can do for hours and not even notice the time pass. Consider this to be a good indicator of something you love doing and that might be pointing toward your calling.

No, really, where does the time go?

PLENTY OF TIME

Make a list of five things you tell yourself you do not have the time for. (Go see a movie/call a certain friend/write a letter to someone who's been on your mind/make art/play music/walk in the woods/travel abroad, etc.) Then, check off the list once you've turned that silly "I don't have time for this" notion on its head.

☐ 1. ....
☐ 2. ....
☐ 3. ....
☐ 4. ....
☐ 5. ....

The two most powerful warriors are patience and time.
—Leo Tolstoy

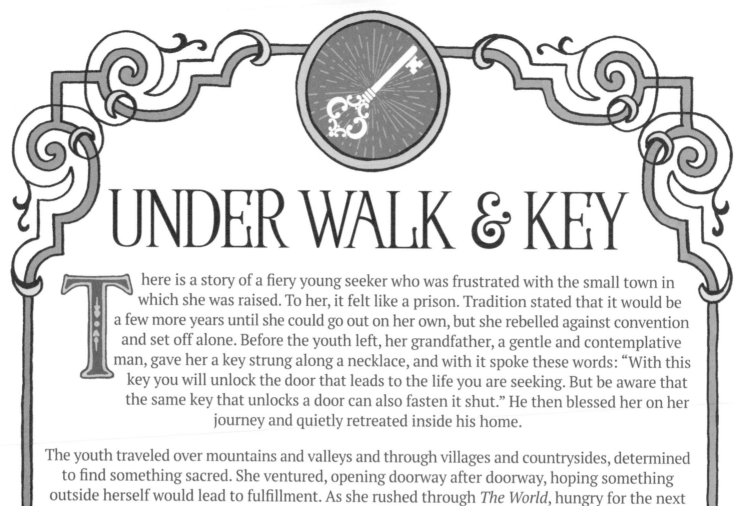

UNDER WALK & KEY

There is a story of a fiery young seeker who was frustrated with the small town in which she was raised. To her, it felt like a prison. Tradition stated that it would be a few more years until she could go out on her own, but she rebelled against convention and set off alone. Before the youth left, her grandfather, a gentle and contemplative man, gave her a key strung along a necklace, and with it spoke these words: "With this key you will unlock the door that leads to the life you are seeking. But be aware that the same key that unlocks a door can also fasten it shut." He then blessed her on her journey and quietly retreated inside his home.

The youth traveled over mountains and valleys and through villages and countrysides, determined to find something sacred. She ventured, opening doorway after doorway, hoping something outside herself would lead to fulfillment. As she rushed through *The World*, hungry for the next experience, she became lost in the labyrinth of her own longing. Exhausted and forlorn, she eventually returned home humbled and heartbroken.

She was met with open arms and tears of joy from her friends and family. Her grandfather was the last to greet her, and did so with the warmest of smiles. "Grandfather," the youth said, "I was too naïve for the world. I saw many things, but I have returned worse than I left." The grandfather took a deep, understanding breath and said: "In my youth, I, too, rushed after knowledge, and I, too, was greeted by wisdom and grace upon my return home. Do not fear, child; there is time for everything—except remaining the same. Come sit by the fire with me. Let us close our eyes and see what we have learned."

Patience Is the Key that opens the door to *The World Within*, an awakened inner life filled with countless treasures and glistening revelations. If *The Key* has found its way into your hand, you are being asked to open doors within yourself, a relationship in your life, or some risk you need to take. The quest of living one's purpose always requires some unique and uncommon door to be unlocked, and *Patience* is the most skilled of all locksmiths. She holds the key to reaching any goal you set, opening opportunities where all other doors remain shut and revealing golden fortunes every step of the way. Eternity is not a time or place reserved for those who have died or passed on; it is happening here and now, always within you. *Patience Is the Key* that gifts you all the time in *The World*.

PATIENCE IS THE KEY

Look around—here we are!
The wild blue yonder! Greener grasses!
You are officially on your way!

And boy, is it a **JOURNEY**.

This one's a marathon, not a sprint.

It has been said that everyone has two jobs in life:
1. To discover what their purpose is.
2. To fulfill that purpose.

I've walked this road before, and you know what I've learned?

If you've ever heard even a whisper of your calling, something unimaginably beautiful is trying to get your attention.

And living your purpose is a process. From where I'm standing, yours looks right on time and exactly as it should be— perfectly imperfect.

We've witnessed the waters and experienced the earth. Where to go next but up in the air . . .

SMALL WONDER

I slept and dreamt that life was joy. I awoke and saw that life was service.
I acted, and behold, service was joy.
—Rabindranath Tagore

As the world turned and bloomed into being, *The Great Mystery* needed a messenger—an enthusiastic and effervescent emissary who could nimbly navigate between the celestial and the terrestrial. Born in the bosom of the rarest of rose-buds, in a meadow atop the most magnificent of mountains next to the swiftest of streams, *Ruby, the Happiest Hummingbird,* hit the air running. Flying so fast, so faithful, and so free, she was the quickest of couriers, checking on creatures large and small, flowers and trees tiny and tall, and hillsides and flatlands rolling and sprawled. Her very presence ensured that Life never became dull but was a joyous and jubilant act ever blossoming with color and creativity. As *Keeper of the Color Red,* Ruby makes her perch at the top of *The Rainbow*—delighting in *The World* like a Sufi poet and a whirling dervish of flight and flower.

"*The Seed* is growing! *The Seed* is growing!" With boundless enthusiasm Ruby happily heralds the coming of Hope and the blossoming of Color.

Ruby knows how to be still while moving so quickly and reminds us to stop and smell the roses and consciously practice presencing joy and delight. Smile wide and smile often as your new friend Ruby takes you under her teeniest of wings to show you the sparkling exuberance that makes each heart flutter.

I AM MY COLOR'S KEEPER

NAME: RUBY
ANIMAL TOTEM: HAPPIEST HUMMINGBIRD
KEEPER OF THE COLOR: RED
VIRTUE: ETERNAL ENTHUSIASM
AFFIRMATION: I BRING JOY TO THE WORLD
KEEPSAKE: WINGS

I just can't wait to watch you color in Ruby as you hover and hum your way through her flight school. In joy!

Walk as if you are kissing the Earth with your feet.
—Thich Nhat Hanh

RUBY

WEIGHT IN VAIN

LEAVE WHAT'S HEAVY BEHIND

What limiting beliefs keep you from flying high? Look at the heavy objects on the right. In the space provided, write the excuse your inner critic gives you that weighs on your soul. And while you're at it, color in the hummingbirds to give them vibrant new wings!

WITHIN-QUIRIES:

What is something someone once said to you that you have been unable to let go of?

On the dotted lines below, write positive affirmations that cut you free from the corresponding old ways of thinking on the next page.

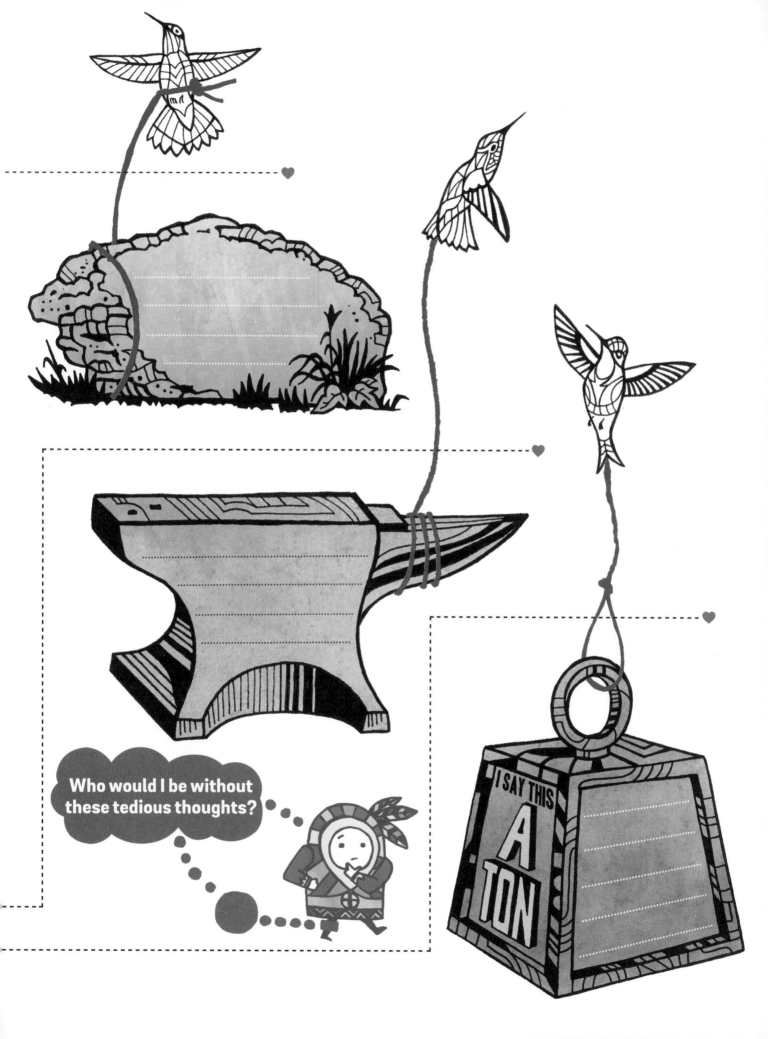

Who would I be without these tedious thoughts?

I SAY THIS A TON

THE LIGHT OF YOUR LIFE

Don't ask what the world needs. Ask what makes you come alive, and go do it.
Because what the world needs is people who have come alive.
—Howard Thurman

DREAMCATCHER EXERCISE: THAT ONE THING

What lights you up? What stirs your soul? What makes your heart flutter? What is that one thing that always brings you back to your heart when you are struggling or challenged? What gets you the most excited when you share about it with others? Is there a beautiful image of your life that you've seen in your mind but perhaps have ignored, discarded, or written off as a fantasy? As crazy or improbable or silly as it may be, feel your heart flutter and write what that thing is in the center of the sun on the next page. Consider that that very thing could be both the nectar that feeds your soul *and* the gift you offer to *The World*!

❖ WITHIN-QUIRIES: ❖

If money and time were no consideration, what would you use your life for?

....

....

....

....

....

....

Just so we're clear:
I'm aiming for your dream.

If you aim at nothing, you'll hit it every time.
—Zig Ziglar

THE FLIGHT OF FANCY

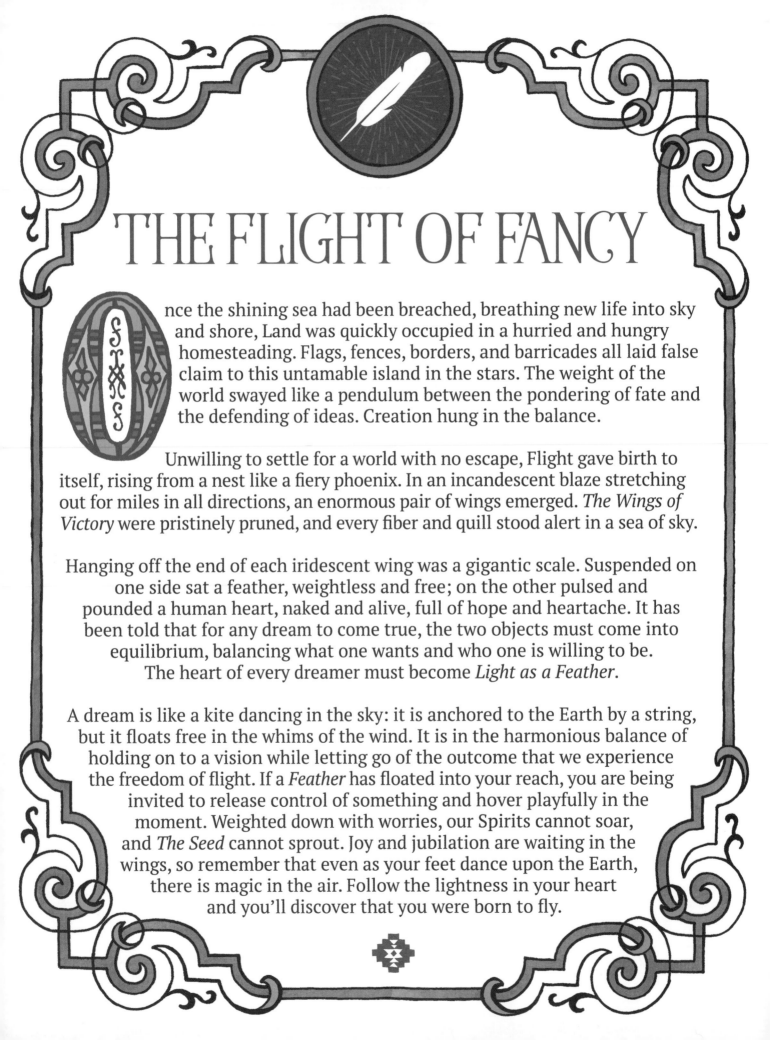

Once the shining sea had been breached, breathing new life into sky and shore, Land was quickly occupied in a hurried and hungry homesteading. Flags, fences, borders, and barricades all laid false claim to this untamable island in the stars. The weight of the world swayed like a pendulum between the pondering of fate and the defending of ideas. Creation hung in the balance.

Unwilling to settle for a world with no escape, Flight gave birth to itself, rising from a nest like a fiery phoenix. In an incandescent blaze stretching out for miles in all directions, an enormous pair of wings emerged. *The Wings of Victory* were pristinely pruned, and every fiber and quill stood alert in a sea of sky.

Hanging off the end of each iridescent wing was a gigantic scale. Suspended on one side sat a feather, weightless and free; on the other pulsed and pounded a human heart, naked and alive, full of hope and heartache. It has been told that for any dream to come true, the two objects must come into equilibrium, balancing what one wants and who one is willing to be. The heart of every dreamer must become *Light as a Feather*.

A dream is like a kite dancing in the sky: it is anchored to the Earth by a string, but it floats free in the whims of the wind. It is in the harmonious balance of holding on to a vision while letting go of the outcome that we experience the freedom of flight. If a *Feather* has floated into your reach, you are being invited to release control of something and hover playfully in the moment. Weighted down with worries, our Spirits cannot soar, and *The Seed* cannot sprout. Joy and jubilation are waiting in the wings, so remember that even as your feet dance upon the Earth, there is magic in the air. Follow the lightness in your heart and you'll discover that you were born to fly.

LIGHT AS A FEATHER

LONG LIVE THE QUEEN

As the bee collects nectar and departs without injuring the flower or its color or fragrance,
so let the sage dwell on earth.
—Buddha

Not all creatures are privy to Nature's private affairs, but let's just say the birds and the bees were chosen for a reason. The Bees, dedicated in their devotion and prodigious in their productivity, were the world's first alchemists. Utilizing hive as hearth, these hardworking honeysmiths transmuted the menial into magic and labor into love. Out of this labor and out of this love a red-hot ambrosial amber poured from Creativity's crucible into a holy and hollow hexagon.
Born out of the birthing of honeycomb was the Most Blessed of Bees and *Keeper of the Color Yellow, Mielle.*

As a magnanimous matriarch, Mielle is concerned only with the health of the whole. To her it's no coincidence that there is no "I" in "team," there are "you" and "I" in "community," and there's "one" in "honey," honey. From slow and steady to busy as a bee, Mielle will give you a productive peek into the art of alchemy. She devotes her entire life to pollinating *The Seed of Hope*, for without it, there would be neither fruit nor flower, and *The World* would be far less colorful. Mielle is grateful for the work she gets to do on Life's behalf. She understands that gratitude, like honey, sweetens all it touches.

I AM MY COLOR'S KEEPER

NAME: MIELLE (ME-EL)
ANIMAL TOTEM: BLESSED BEE
KEEPER OF THE COLOR: YELLOW
VIRTUE: POLLINATING GRATITUDE
AFFIRMATION:
I GIVE THANKS TO ALL WORKING ON MY BEHALF
KEEPSAKE: ELIXIR

I'm a bee–Keeper of Color!
Can you do me a favor and color in Mielle and follow her royal orders? Do as she says, and everything will bee okay.

Life is the flower for which love is the honey.
—Victor Hugo

MIELLE

REVIVE THE HIVE

When you go in search of honey, you must expect to get stung by bees.
—Joseph Joubert

A STING OPERATION

When the hive has gone lifeless and gray or when the honey ceases to flow, never forget you have a life-transforming fire called inspiration inside you. This alchemy literally revives the hive. Watch how giving color to *The World Within* harmonizes the world around you. Using the chart below, fill in each cell of the honeycomb as a paint-by-number to see what all the buzz is about.

0 - WHITE 1 - RED 2 - ORANGE 3 - INDIGO
4 - GREEN 5 - BLUE 6 - PURPLE
7 - BLACK

> This really is none of your beeswax.

❖ WITHIN-QUIRIES: ❖

> What is something you feel stung by that hasn't fully healed?

> Where in your life are you afraid to stir up a hornet's nest?

Hope is the only bee that makes honey without flowers.
—Robert Green Ingersoll

HELPER BEES

Aerodynamically, the bumblebee shouldn't be able to fly,
but the bumblebee doesn't know it, so it goes on flying anyway.
—Mary Kay Ash

THE BEE'S KNEES

Who are the people in your life whom you can always count on or who have been magical aids in altering your life? In the corresponding boxes on the next page, write down their names and color in your favorite helper bees who remind you how sweet life is.

 WITHIN-QUIRIES:

What adds sweetness and honey to your life?

How have you contributed to making someone else's dream come true?

Friends are the siblings God never gave us.
—Mencius

HELPER BEE #1

HELPER BEE #2

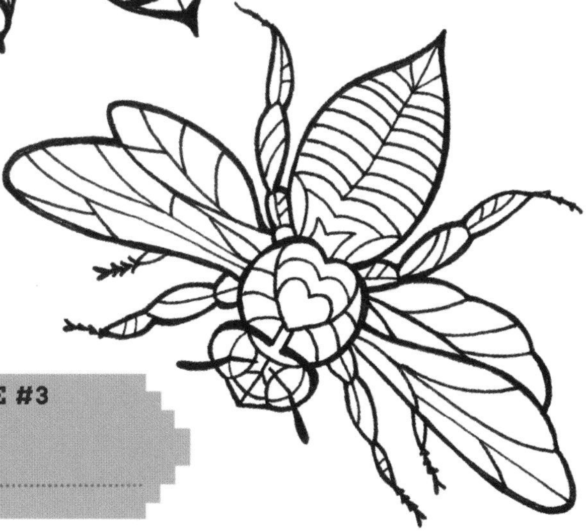

HELPER BEE #3

HELPER BEE #4

HELPER BEE #5

Beauty is in the eyes of the bee-holder.

SUITE AS HONEY

There once was a river named Productivity, and it was granted the task of carving out a beautiful, awe-inspiring canyon. Given thousands of years and endless rains to work with, the river labored tirelessly for centuries, never once ceasing to flow. From time to time, Productivity encountered boulders and fallen trees, mountains and uphill climbs, yet still it trickled forward. One day it hit a wall, and the exhausted river became a lake. It lay flat and unmoving—peaceful, but stagnant. Productivity had become mechanical and meaningless, and the once bubbly river had lost its joy.

The Great Mystery wept at this sight. "All this hard work," she thought, "deserves a reward." And so she employed her most trusted Alchemists to concoct a nectar so pure, so perfectly sweet, so unabashedly ambrosial that it would be a food fit for the Gods. It would be a life-restoring wine of wonder that never soured, even in stagnation. The longer it steeped, the sweeter it became.

With a secret recipe that only Nature knew, the Alchemists formulated *The Elixir of Eternity*. What is this secret recipe, you ask? Love—the Love of Life itself.

To someone living their purpose, nothing is more fulfilling or quenches the deepest of thirsts better than honest work well done; this is the fire that melts all else away. It ennobles the soul, invigorates the body, and sweetens the spirit. A devoted heart becomes Life's laboratory—a place where it can do its work, entrust its secrets, and reveal its cure for all ills. Through this forge of faith, anyone can turn the most challenging of lessons into pure gold.

If *The Elixir* has been poured into your life's cup, you are encouraged to drink in the concoction of circumstances being offered to you. Whatever the situation, seemingly good or bad, it is medicine for you. Life is a great distillery where wisdom is always on tap and love is served as a perfectly prescribed potion for YOU. Let's raise a glass so you can pour your heart out.

THE ELIXIR OF ETERNITY

A shell to sing out, a key to open *Worlds Within*, and a feather to fly?
You are one blossoming dreamer!

Look how far you've come!

Look how far you have left to go!

Look how far-out Life is.

When you lose the sense of familiar groundedness, keep letting go, and you'll discover there's freedom to float between the big, beautiful vision and delighting in the details.

YOU ARE HERE

Let's take a breath.

And then, a smoothie break.

Life can be hard, but this honey sure does sweeten the sting.

The good, the bad, the fun, and the frustrating are all part of a delicious recipe called *The Great Mystery*, where there are always free refills.

We've gone over, we've gone under. We've even gone up above. Now we're about to go *in*.

HONOR THE INNER

Be a lamp unto yourself.
—Buddha

Out beyond the notions of right and wrong—where seeking stops, where knowingness knows and Being becomes—there sat a small, unassuming hill, a round, grassy pregnant-belly of earth that had been covered by blankets of snow during a long, enduring winter. And in that belly there was a hole—a burrow, actually, a navel to a deep, underground world where *The Seed of Hope* was said to be buried. Coiled up cozily next to a flickering flame was *Honor, the Badger of Brilliance.* A natural-born wanderer, Honor had retreated from *The World as We Know It,* vowing not to return until *The Seed* had sprouted or he had become enlightened. So at the dawn of a Cosmic Spring, the sun grew warmer and gently melted away the snow. It tiptoed down into Honor's tunnel and wrapped him in an all-enveloping light. Knowing *The Great Mystery* had sent the literal light of day, Honor awakened to his purpose. A daring dreamer, intrepid inquisitor, and *Keeper of the Color Purple,* Honor traveled far and wide and searched the world upside down and inside out to uncover the perfect conditions for *The Seed* to grow. He knew the tips of every tree and the fringe of every fern. He knew the bend in every brook and the nature in every nook. Honor never feared digging in and doing the work, nor shying away from tunnel vision.

Honor is a master of foraging and forging his path. He is here to help us boldly uncover, unearth, and ultimately understand who we are and where we wish to go. With this understanding we can honor ourselves, *The World Within,* and *The Great Mystery* that governs it all. Honor lives by J. R. R. Tolkien's belief that "not all who wander are lost," but if and when we are, we can all use a little guiding light. Thankfully, this badger's calling is to be one such beacon.

I AM MY COLOR'S KEEPER

NAME: HONOR
ANIMAL TOTEM: THE BADGER OF BRILLIANCE
KEEPER OF THE COLOR: PURPLE
VIRTUE: TRUSTING INTUITION
AFFIRMATION: I AM A LIGHT IN THE WORLD
KEEPSAKE: LANTERN

THIS WAY

I don't want to keep badgering you, but I would be Honored if you'd color in your new friend here as he guides us through these next steps.

You uncover what is when you get rid of what isn't.
—Buckminster Fuller

HONOR

THE SHADOW OF A DOUBT

Worry often gives a small thing a big shadow.
—Proverb

YOUR OWN WORST ENEMY

In life—and certainly in dream-finding—you will be faced with obstacles or blocks to your path. Sometimes you can go around them—but sometimes the only way out is through. Honor understands that many a would-be trailblazer is often stopped in his or her tracks by being scared of his or her own shadow. So that fear does not obstruct our progress, we are going to stare your shadow in the face by literally drawing it out of hiding. The following exercise is here to help you turn toward "your shadow," "your wound," or an "inner demon" to discover where it lives and what it is asking of you.

Step 1: Pick one of your inner adversaries, a habitual tendency that consistently interferes with your life. Is it Doubt? Shame? Laziness? Boredom? Jealousy? Anger, Anxiety, or Depression? Whatever it is, consider that until you confront it, it will block your passageway to freedom.

Step 2: In the space below, we are going to get into its world. Describe this shadowy self in as much detail as you can (you can use an alternate journal page if you need to). What does it look like? Does it have two eyes or one? Does it have teeth, claws, horns, or fur? Does it breathe fire? Shoot lasers? In what situations does it rear its head? What does it want from you? What does it believe? What is it protecting you from? How does it lure you off your path?

Step 3: On the following page, in *The Gray Area* provided, draw as best you can the character you see. Once you have brought it out of the shadows and into the light, you are free to turn the page and proceed on this adventure.

Describe your inner adversary here.

Knowing your own darkness is the best method for dealing with the darknesses of other people.
—Carl Jung

THE HEART WITHIN THE HEART

What lies behind us and what lies before us are tiny matters compared to what lies within us.
—Ralph Waldo Emerson

LOVE SPELUNKING

It has been said that "the longest journey we each must take is the eighteen inches from the head to the heart." It's amazing what you will find if you just keep searching, and only in searching can we see the difference between the darkness of the unknown and the darkness of fear itself. Both reside in *The World Within*. A secret of secrets offered to the boldest of the brave is that *The World Within* can be illuminated, explored, and made conscious. It requires those willing to patiently plow the rocky, infertile soil of neglect into their vibrant inner kingdoms, where fruitful orchards, majestic temples, and measureless wisdom await. To honor your journey inward, color in *The World Within* on the next page. See if you can find not only hidden treasures but some kindred *Keepers* as well. As you seek, so shall you find!

◈ WITHIN-QUIRIES: ◈

What are you hiding from the world?

How do you move from your head to your heart?

And you? When will you begin that long journey into yourself?
—Rumi

LIGHT OF MINE

"Seek and ye shall find." It is said again and again in a thousand different tongues, and upon innumerable different paths. In the bee-buzzing, siren-screeching, hare-racing empire of opportunities, it can often prove difficult to discern which road leads to which where.

When one speaks of illumination and enlightenment, one also speaks of darkness. The loneliness of an unexplored soul calls out for the bright light that only awareness can offer. Thankfully, *The Lantern of Luminosity* is the dazzling and brilliant response to every such cry in the night. It is the lamp of your own intuition, the sun and star within your own heart. Each of us carries a lamp of personal truth lit long ago by *The Great Mystery*. It is a means to find our way through *The World Within* so that we may reunite with our glorious origins.

If *The Lantern*'s glow has cast its friendly flicker into your life, know that you are being asked to hold it high and spread its light far and wide. Perhaps you are being called to see what lies hidden in the unexamined nooks and crannies of a situation, to light the way so others may see, to walk in peaceful vigil through the darkest hours, or to remember that when you shine, so does *The World as We Know It*. Fear not, for this lantern's flame can never be extinguished, so let there be light!

THE LANTERN OF LUMINOSITY

The soul speaks in a very peculiar language. It speaks in symbols and subtleties, mysteries and metaphor, omens and ordeals. The soul speaks through our resolve to listen.

But if we choose not to listen, if we ignore or disregard our calling, our unlived dream atrophies. The call then becomes dim and distant and desaturates *The World* from the inside out. Ambiguity arises, and confusion creeps in. *The Keepers of Color* refer to this phenomenon as *The Gray Area*.

Spawned in the unconscious, far beyond the shadow of a doubt, *The Gray Area* is a no-man's-land where lies live, violence festers, and cowardice hides. It's relentless. It's patient. It's irreverent and brash. Like an amnesia to aliveness, it slips in little by little, sucking the life and color out of all it touches and rendering *The World* bored with apathy.

Without respect or reverence for *The Great Mystery* and without a sense of connection or responsibility to *The World Within*, *The Gray Area* became a lawless realm where unthinkable thoughts gave voice to unspeakable words, which permitted unimaginable realities. *The World as We Know It* was no place like home.

A shrewd and sharp-witted dragon named *Kōan* lived inside *The Gray Area*. Kōan was an*dragon*ous, both male and female, the protector and a prisoner of this lifeless realm. Kōan was the beast within *The Gray Area*'s bottomless belly. His eyes were made of mirrors, his teeth were pointing fingers, and her cunning tongue spoke in proverb and paradox.

Once colorful and bright, Kōan had lived for eons feasting on imagination and interest. Kōan posed wild, insatiable questions that inspired wild and wondrous answers, each one more delicious and nourishing than the last. But slowly, as *The Gray Area* spread, so, too, did diversion and disorder. Many began ignoring Kōan's inward inquiries and as his belly roared with hunger, he sank his teeth into *The Rainbow of Remembrance*, consuming the only color and creativity he knew remained. Each *Keeper* living blissfully within the once-vibrant world was forced to flee or face the invading darkness. The Kingdom was in peril, because the world had become deficient of dreamers.

Dark soon became darker, stark grew even starker, and all seemed lost. *The Gray Area* had become so rampant and widespread that *The Web of Life* and the balance that made existence possible was pushed to its very brink. No one was safe from this paralyzing affliction, and no side or stance was sheltered. The pacifists, the optimists, and the do-gooders all would have to answer Kōan's ultimate questions: "Who are you, and what have you come here to do?"

Meanwhile, deep below the surface, a quiet transformation was taking place. Shrouded in darkness, *The Seed of Hope* sat in stillness underneath it all, quietly observing the distant clamor above. While *The World* was being divided, *The Seed* alone held an ancient wisdom and the power to restore. Tucked safely away within *The Seed* was a dream, a one-of-a-kind vision complete with instructions and inspiration for the dream's realization.

The Keepers knew, however, that while *The Seed* contained the dream, it was not the dream itself. They knew that in order for a new life to be born, *The Seed* had to perish. *The Seed* must learn to trust Life, to surrender so fully to *The Great Mystery* that it is willing to come undone and allow a beautiful and miraculous process to unfold through it.

Though wise and wondrous, this process is not guaranteed. Not all seeds sprout, nor does every seed realize its fruits. But all seeds—just like all beings—do carry Hope.

The dream, if realized, could bring Love and Light to these dismal times, but it required beings to descend into the darkness and discover *The Seed* inside them. To *The Keepers*, there was nothing more sacred than this inward journey.

So their calls for consciousness continued, ringing out across the land. *The Keepers* were searching for custodians of Color—anyone who was willing, quite simply and quite honorably, to believe in themselves, to come as they were, hopeful yet humbled, and to step faithfully forward through the darkness of the unknown into the promise of the new.

Okay, my friend. You've been thoroughly prepped. Pack a bag and some snacks—we're going in.

"*The Belly of the Beast,*"
"*The Valley of the Shadow of Death,*"
"*The Gray Area*"—
it's all the same to me. (Gulp.)

It certainly isn't pretty, but we can't get through without going in. (Big gulp.)

The Gray Area is here for a reason.

I've tried running from it, tiptoeing around it, and straight-up ignoring it—but none of that will get us through.

Because the tighter we hold on to our fears and the more stubbornly we close our eyes to our truth, the grayer *The Gray Area* becomes.

YOU
ARE
HERE

So, we've got to go in, ready to look at our own contradictions, conflicts, and inconsistencies. Staring uncertainty in the face is not easy, but there is wisdom in the paradox.

To enter *The Gray Area*, you'll need to trust in *The Great Mystery*. I'm not usually much of a daredevil (aside from my fashion sense), but you and your dream are helping me put on my fearless face.

Up until now, we've been brave enough to go in; let's see if we're brave enough to go *through*. I mean, we don't have to. Maybe this whole adventure is just a silly idea. Maybe *The Gray Area* isn't so bad after all. There are probably plenty of other things you could be doing rather than turning the page . . .

BEHIND CLOSED DOORS

In order to cause a shadow to disappear, you must shine light on it.
—Shakti Gawain

BEST-KEPT SECRETS

Phew! That was too close for comfort. As we begin to descend into *The Gray Area*, it's important to understand that whatever you are afraid of lives in here—but whatever you hope to find also lives in here. On the next page, you will notice three *Doorways of Denial*. Behind each doorway lies a secret of yours, something you are hiding or feel ashamed of or guilty about. You can think of them as big, cosmic "I can't believe I did that"s. Usually they each contain an aspect of yourself that you don't want to look at or something you hope will go away. As you ponder these moments, try to see what led you to those mistakes. What desire was wanting to be fulfilled, and what lessons did you ultimately learn? Answer the first set of questions below, and once you have, color in the corresponding doorway to mark it as unlocked. Then, after answering the second set of questions, color in the corresponding gem outside each doorway, signifying the hidden treasure each "mistake" taught you.

WITHIN-QUIRIES:

What three secrets are behind your Doorways of Denial?

1 ....
2 ....
3 ....

What lessons or treasures did they ultimately bestow upon you?

....

....

....

Experience is a hard teacher because she gives the test first, the lesson afterward.
—Vernon Law

THE MASKS WE WEAR

Love takes off the masks that we fear we cannot live without and know we cannot live within.
—James Baldwin

THIS TIME IT'S PERSONA

As we venture deeper into *The Gray Area*, we begin to see some of the things we've hidden from the light of day—most notably who we are. The word "persona" means "stage mask" in Latin. Wearing a physical mask affords the wearer both freedom and anonymity—a space to roam between realms, hidden behind a veil of secrecy. We, too, walk between worlds by wearing the masks of different personalities around certain people and social circles within our lives. Color in the masks on the following page and answer the questions below to see how alter egos may present themselves in your life and what you may be hiding beneath them.

 WITHIN-QUIRIES:

What persona, character quality, or way you behave is uniquely present when you are:

with relatives?

with your partner/spouse?

with someone you are trying to impress?

with wealthy people?

with someone less fortunate than you?

with a group of only men?

with a group of only women?

with someone who adores you?

with someone who irritates you?

by yourself?

Man is least himself when he talks in his own person.
Give him a mask, and he will tell you the truth.
—Oscar Wilde

STAY OR WEAVE

*We are the weavers, we are the web
We are the spiders and we are the thread.*
—Shekinah Moutainwater

Whispers tell a tale of a spindler who spun herself and the first story into existence. As it's been told, the fabric of the cosmos was woven with two different strands known as *The Threads of Time*. Intelligence was the first thread, knitted with knowledge and discernment, and Integrity the second, wound by strength and virtue. Together these fibers formed an unbreakable union of Love and Trust. Back and forever forth, *The Threads of Time* stitched together the most exquisite living quilt, known as *The Web of Life*.

This perfectly ordered *Web* held all of life in place, spanning over *The World* like a giant dome and beneath it like a supportive safety net. It connected each and every being to one another, to *The Web* itself, and, most important, to *The Great Mystery*. At the very center of *The Web* was an eight-pointed star. Out of these eight points grew eight spindly legs, and there, sitting in eternal presence at the center of all of existence, was *Uru, the Spider Spindler*, and *Keeper of the Color Silver*.

Drawing the colorful yarns of your past and looping them with filaments of your future, Uru watches as you weave your life into being. When your life is coming apart at the seams, she invites you to consider whether you are a spider sitting atop your own careful creation or you have fallen prey to a trap you yourself have lain. Fear not—Uru is here to toss you a lifeline and to remind you: "We are the spider and also its thread—our lives are our actions and words we have said. Let us remember from where we came; in the great *Web of Life* we are one and the same."

I AM MY COLOR'S KEEPER

NAME: URU (OOH-ROO)

ANIMAL TOTEM: THE SPIDER SPINDLER

KEEPER OF THE COLOR: SILVER

VIRTUE: WEAVING WORLDS

AFFIRMATION:

I AM RESPONSIBLE FOR ALL THAT I CREATE

KEEPSAKE: ENDLESS KNOT

Don't get caught by the fact that she's a spider—Uru is here to help! So suspend any judgments and color away, and let her take you for a spin through her web of wisdom!

The bird a nest, the spider a web, man friendship.
—William Blake

URU

CONNECT THE DON'TS

TANGLED UP IN YOU

Oftentimes we can judge *The World* for being a mixed-up place, but our own lives aren't as simple as we may let on. Through this exercise we will see where we've deviated from our own sense of integrity and how we can get caught in a web of our own mistakes. Answer the questions below, and when prompted, connect the corresponding dots on the next page.

Karmic Bonus: Where appropriate, work to clean up any entanglements in your life.

WITHIN-QUIRIES:

Have you ever . . .

		Answer Yes or No	If Yes, connect dots:
1.	Lied?	1.	1 to 12
2.	Numbed yourself with food, substances, media, etc.?	2.	2 to 13
3.	Thought of yourself as better or less than another?	3.	3 to 7
4.	Been destructive or harmful (through words or actions)?	4.	4 to 8
5.	Put off something very important?	5.	5 to 10
6.	Held resentment or envy toward another?	6.	6 to 11
7.	Worked so much that you lost sight of what was important?	7.	7 to 14
8.	Taken anything that was not yours?	8.	8 to 12
9.	Sought your own gratification while ignoring another?	9.	9 to 13
10.	Became attached to the idea of having someone or something?	10.	10 to 14
11.	Gossiped about someone?	11.	11 to 13
12.	Not asked for what you needed or wanted for fear of a no?	12.	12 to 2
13.	Spent more time/energy/money than you had?	13.	13 to 14
14.	Sought the admiration of others for validation?	14.	14 to 3

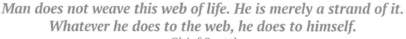

A WEB OF WHYS

DREAMCATCHER EXERCISE: 100 QUESTIONS

In Michael Gelb's book *How to Think Like Leonardo da Vinci*, he encourages us to tap into our inquisitive and childlike nature, to question everything—even our questions themselves. He offers us the following exercise. You'll want to give yourself some time—I'd say forty-five minutes to an hour, and if you can, try to complete it all in one sitting. Using the web on the next page, we are going to make a list of one hundred questions. Whatever comes to mind is totally fine. "Why is the sky blue?" "What is the meaning of Life?" "Why not twenty questions?"

Usually, the first few dozen questions will seem trite or arbitrary. That's totally normal. Keep going. About halfway through, you'll probably see some themes begin to emerge. The homestretch is usually where the unexpected inquiries start to arise. Once you've completed this task, review your list of questions and choose ten that you find most compelling. In the space below, rank them in importance from 1 to 10. THEN, from those ten, find the biggest, boldest, most soul-stirring question. This question will undoubtedly be related to your calling or purpose. Finally, in the center of the web, write down your word or phrase for *The Great Mystery* (i.e., God, Spirit, Creator, the Universe). Can you see that the answers to all your questions are somehow connected to that term?

What are the ten most important questions you have about Life?

1. ....
2. ....
3. ....
4. ....
5. ....
6. ....
7. ....
8. ....
9. ....
10. ....

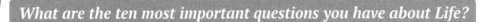

What question is your life about answering?

1. ....

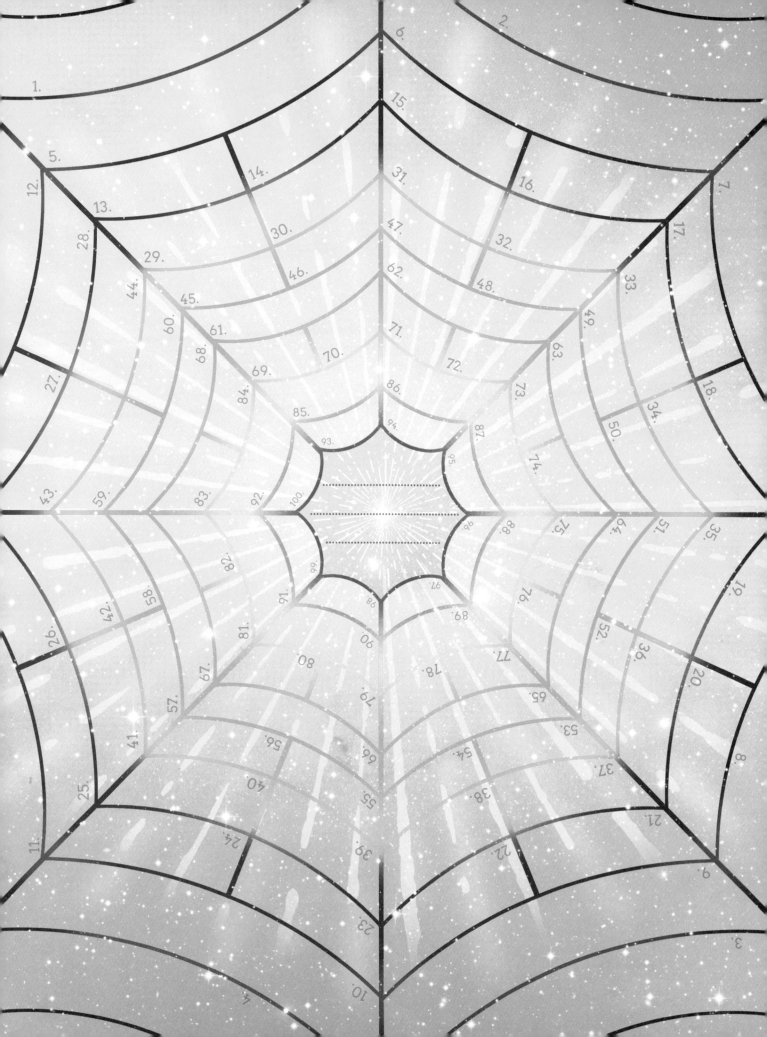

TIED. TOGETHER.

The Great Mystery is a tale told without beginning or end. It is a pathless path trodden between known and unknown lands, where Spirit mingles with matter and where what seems to matter does not matter at all. Nature is a stage for this ballet of opposites. The Sun and the Rain, predator and prey, growth and decay all dance in dichotomy.

In order to teach its enigmatic ways, *The Great Mystery* saw each being as a child and gifted them a toy, a paradox to play with, a *Keepsake* that required holding two seemingly opposing truths, one in each hand.

This compassionate craftsmanship was tied in an eternal twist known as *The Knot of This World*. A boomerang of cause and effect, *The Knot* gives the gift of creativity, granting everyone the ability to perpetually make, unmake, and remake the lives they choose to experience.

If *The Knot* has woven its way into your relationships, you are being asked to look at where you might be fettered to an old idea or fastened to a stubborn belief that encumbers your frolic or freedom. Are you stringing yourself or others along? Are you raveled in continual drama? *The Knot of This World* is not a bond of restraint but rather a twist of fate. It is the rope of relationship and the kindred connection we have with all things. It is the independence of interdependence. To hold this knot in your hand is to be holding hands with all of Life, for we are all always connected.

KNOT OF THIS WORLD

A GRAVE ENCOUNTER

Unbeing dead isn't being alive.
—e. e. cummings

DREAMCATCHER EXERCISE: SET IN STONE

Okay, let's really face it—there's one thing most of us are scared of: death. When the thought of death arises, most people are actually afraid of the LIFE they have not lived. Rather than waiting to deal with death in the last possible moments, ancient cultures would place death in the center of Life—not as something morbid or frightening but as a natural part of *The Great Mystery*. So, let's practice dying. We are going to imagine that you died today. Suddenly. Unexpectedly. On the next page, we're going to write your epitaph as an obituary. Be honest and generous with your praise and truthful about your shortcomings. What haven't you accomplished, found, or experienced? Oftentimes staring death in the face can reveal what is most important to you. If you died today, what would you leave behind, unlived? See if this exercise breathes life back into your dream or calling.

What are your three biggest regrets?

1. ....
2. ....
3. ....

How does an awareness of death inspire you to live?

....
....
....

Even death is not to be feared by one who has lived wisely.
—Buddha

HERE LIES

_____,
YOUR NAME

a beloved _____, _____, and
THREE RELATIONAL ROLES (i.e., FATHER, SISTER, DAUGHTER, FRIEND, TEACHER, YOGI)

_____.

As a/an _____, _____ was a hard worker and
JOB TITLE   YOUR NAME

accomplished many great things, including _____,
LIST THREE ACCOLADES

_____, and _____.

_____ also had a special gift of_____.
HE/SHE   A UNIQUE TALENT OF YOURS

_____ was well loved by friends and family, who knew
HE/SHE

_____ as _____, _____, and
HIM/HER   THREE WORDS YOUR FRIENDS OR LOVED ONES WOULD USE TO DESCRIBE YOU

_____.

_____ leaves behind the dream of becoming a/an
HE/SHE

_____,
A VOCATION OR TITLE YOU HAVE ALWAYS WANTED

including a/an_____, a/an_____,
THREE PROJECTS YOU WISH TO ONE DAY COMPLETE

and a/an _____ that were never fully realized.

_____ final words were: "_____."
HIS/HER   WORDS YOU LIVE BY OR WISH YOU DID

LOVE
EACH
DAY
AND YOU'LL
NEVER TURN
OLD
OR
GRAY

BENEFIT OF THE DOUBT

Long ago, *The Great Mystery* created two twin kingdoms named *Yin* and *Yang*, one side dark, the other side light. Male, Female. This way and that. *Yin* and *Yang* were separated by a great serpentine creature named *Kōan*. Kōan was something between a snake and a dragon, still unformed and becoming. Kōan was both male and female, and was much like a riddle waiting to be solved, taking one form as a question was asked and another upon its being answered. Kōan's very purpose was to ask "What is the purpose?" His long, scaly body separated the two powerful kingdoms like a great, winding wall of wisdom. Each of his eyes was a crystal-clear mirror. One reflected how you saw yourself, and the other how he saw you. Catching a glimpse of her gaze left most terrified, some mystified, and everyone in awe.

Natives from either kingdom could ask Kōan anything, and he always answered with a question, a rhetorical and inquisitive puzzle for the mind that only the heart could solve. These riddles were designed to provoke ardent analysis, fiery dialogue, and, in their most impassioned form, doubt. His queries were his lair, and here was where *The Seed of Hope* was buried. A life-renewing failsafe for times of darkness, *The Seed* patiently waited to be discovered, yearning to be watered and given light. Kōan guarded the soil in which *The Seed* was buried, and his thick, torpid body would not budge without an answer that would bring peace to her inquiring heart.

But very few truly wanted to answer what she was asking of them. Because of this, Kōan and her questions were mostly misunderstood, misappropriated, and even abused. You see, the problems of *The World* WERE her questions. They reflected *The World* back at itself. The violence, devastation, and unthinkable atrocities all asked, "Is this the life you want?" Without answers and without attempts, *The World* spun in endless uncertainty, chasing its own tail and whisking *The Gray Area* into even greater turmoil, until one day the eerie and unanswered silence finally responded, "How will this story end?"

I AM YOUR COLOR'S KEEPER

NAME: KOAN (KOH-AHN)

TOTEM: DRAGON OF DOUBT

KEEPER OF THE COLOR: GRAY

VIRTUE: DARING TO ASK

AFFIRMATION:
WHAT'S MY PURPOSE?

KEEPSAKE: ?

KŌAN

POINTING FINGERS

The more hidden the venom, the more dangerous it is.
—Margaret of Valois

GET OUT THE POISON

To admit we have made mistakes, that we are scared and that our best-laid plans have failed—sometimes epically—allows us to liberate ourselves from the constricting binds of denial and blame by acknowledging how much we do not know, how much we cannot see, and how much we're not actually in control of. On the next page, let's color in Kōan so as not to be eaten by our excuses or devoured by our defensiveness. Just like Kōan's mirroring stare, *The World* is inviting you to look at it, face it, and heal what needs the unique medicine of your love. And while we're at it, let's point those compassionate fingers toward the mirror and know that's who has the ability and the responsibility to realize our dreams.

What are you avoiding?

List your five favorite excuses for why you haven't achieved your dream.

1.
2.
3.
4.
5.

If your daily life seems poor, do not blame it;
blame yourself that you are not poet enough to call forth its riches;
for the Creator, there is no poverty.
—Rainer Maria Rilke

AND ZEN IT HAPPENED

Nothing ever goes away until it has taught us what we need to know.
—Pema Chodron

ENSŌ IT IS

There are times in our lives when we get stuck. We find ourselves back in the same exact place, learning the same exact lesson. Most often we plow through, sidestep, or ignore it. We do whatever we can to make it go away. In doing so, we fail to learn what's being asked of us. Yet underneath it, all something is always there, holding us. In these moments when all seems lost, it's good to know there is always a way—a way we often forget about. What's needed is surrender and grace. Just like patience and joy, this space of peace and tranquillity has been in us all along. When we continue to swirl in circles or keep hitting the same walls, no amount of diving in, pushing through, or striving for will do. To let go into *The Great Mystery* is to trust that we will be held, knowing it's safe to fall.

◈ WITHIN-QUIRIES: ◈

What are you letting go of?

What do you trust in?

Don't seek, don't search, don't ask, don't knock, don't demand—relax.
—Osho

YOU
ARE
HERE

BE HOLD & BE HELD

Hello, my child.
I am so glad you are here.
You have worked so hard and come so far.
Your laboring has done all it can.
Now you are simply asked to REST.

Allow me to fill you with Life.
Do not forget that you rise each day to seek me.
Do not forget that you work each day to know me.
Do not forget who calls you home to Rest.
It is Life. The Great Mystery.
Rest.

Live the dream of your own becoming.
The one I whisper to you.
The one I have placed inside your heart.
Give all your actions to me.

It is okay not to know.
Get comfortable with that truth.
I am holding you.
Close your eyes; do not be afraid.
Rest.

Give me your faith.
It does not have to be faith in a God or a leader or some practice or principle.
Put your faith in the journey itself.

Stop pursuing your goals, your ideas, your visions of yourself.
All of them lead you to you, not me.
Put down your tools, unplug your machines, turn off the noise.
Stop striving to be; you already are.
Rest.
Everything will be okay.

Rest in the mystery that drums your own heart and twirls the planet upon which you play.
In there are the simplest instructions on how to live:
1) Love
2) Rest

You take care of the loving.
I'll take care of the REST.

UNDER HER WINGS

Love is an endless mystery, for it has nothing else to explain it.
—Rabindranath Tagore

It is said that no mortal can truly know *The Great Mystery*, that it is concealed beneath a veil of endless forms, hidden in the decency of darkness, where Life and death, desire and dream each arise only to disappear again. But the bravest of souls who have dared to pull back the veil all claim to have encountered a woman. They say that though they could not see her eyes, they knew they were looking straight through them—nor could they see her heart, because its brilliance would blind them. All one could see, it was said, were her wings.

Runa the Raven was Queen of the Night and Doula of the Day, a shape-shifting Goddess who cradled the promise of all potential within her womb. In the loving embrace of her wine-black wings was where *The Seed of Hope* nestled and grew, where babies curled up carefree and stars swam in the ocean of night. Runa was cloaked by *The Illuminated Darkness*, a glowing, radiant, pregnant dark that brimmed with creativity and was completely suffused with light.

Like an exotic bird flashing its tail or ornately colored collar, Runa walks in a decorative display of beauty and wonder, sometimes modest, sometimes lavish, but always with an otherworldly elegance. The sun resting on the snow, the mountains cresting beyond the moon, the sky skipping along the sea are all jewels upon her gown. You'll see her everywhere you look, though she is invisible. This is her magic. This is *The Great Mystery*.

I AM MY COLOR'S KEEPER

NAME: RUNA (ROO-NAH)
ANIMAL TOTEM: RAVEN OF REVELATION
KEEPER OF THE COLOR: BLACK
VIRTUE: MYSTERY IN MOTION
AFFIRMATION: I REST IN PEACE
KEEPSAKE: SEED

Shhhh . . .
I'm practicing my
shape-shifting.

I will love the light, for it shows me the way,
yet I will endure the darkness, for it shows me the stars.
—Og Mandino

RUNA

WOMB TO GROW

Precious child of light, you are a seed in a vast and magnificent Universe. Just as a tiny seed resting within the Earth contains the entire tree in potential, you, too, contain wonders beyond your current form. When one gazes upon a seed, there are no signs of the roots, stem, flowers, or fruit. These features, so fundamental to a tree, develop only when nurtured—and the same can be said for you.

You do not need to know how to become a tree. The life within you already exists within The Seed, and you simply must learn how to tend to it. There are spaces within you that are quiet, still, and un-touched, fertile darkness, places of preparation, free from noise and knowledge. Connect with these spaces. Dwell within them. Commune and cultivate the soil of your soul.

In the exercise below, we are going to begin a call-and-response dialogue. You are going to play both Asker and Answerer, Sower and Seed. In the first part, knowing The Seed contains your dream and the wisdom to grow into its fully realized form, what question would you like to have it answer? Where in your life or in living your calling are you seeking guidance? Write your question below. Then, listen closely to The Seed's answer and write down what you hear. You cannot do this incorrectly.

For the second part, remember: You and The Seed are inseparable. You are friends forever, under my wings, held by Life itself. The Seed believes in you fully, and neither one of you can become who you were meant to be without the other. Knowing this, what question is The Seed asking you? Again, listen closely and write The Seed's question and then your response below. My marvelous, beautiful child, do not be afraid, for you are not alone. The humble and forgiving Earth supports you, the radiant light of the Sun welcomes you with open arms, and my mysterious wings, drenched in Love, are wrapped all around you. You are safe to become.

SEEDING IS BELIEVING

Legend speaks of a jewel that sparkles with such holy purity, with such a rare and remarkable shine that to catch a glimpse of it is to stare into *The Great Mystery*. It is said that no fire can burn it, though to know it is to be aflame; that no stone can crush it, though to become it is to be polished and refined.

The Seed of Hope is more than just a seed—it is a prism that contains a spark that contains a promise. This divine germ contains the entire blueprint for your dream realized, and it lies resting in *The World Within* your heart.

The Seed is an infinite and eternal treasure living within you, an heirloom to your story yet to be told. It can never be uprooted, though it can be ignored or forgotten. Just as a single grain can fill an entire field and feed many hungry mouths, you, too, contain the ability to grow, multiply, and share the abundant and diverse riches within you.

If *The Seed of Hope* has sprouted into your life, your task is to tend to it. Awaken it and give it life by creating the perfect conditions for both you and it to flourish. Finding this inner gift, however, is not your dream realized nor your purpose fulfilled but simply that which shines the way to and through *The Great Mystery*.

Whether your dream is just beginning to stir or you can feel the fullness of it realized, it lives within this *Seed*, waiting in the quiet soil of your soul for the rains of your attention and the sunshine of your Love. Your calling, your passions, and your purpose are all promises in potential, and you must grow toward the light of your destiny!

So sow this *Seed* and become a tree, a garden, an orchard.
Harvest your Hope and share the endless
bounty of *The World Within* you.

THE SEED OF HOPE

I'm going to just say it: WOW. You are here! You looked your shadow in the face. (So tricky!) You learned about *The Web of Life* and the interconnectedness of all things. (That's deep!)

You learned to let go and surrender, trusting that you are ultimately held in the loving hands of something so much bigger. (I mean, isn't that the meaning of being just fine?)

And you got to see yourself growing through the eyes of a seed.

(How could I do anything BUT believe in you?)

Keep your ears open. *The Seed* will continue to speak through your life in the most obvious or unexpected places. We're heading back up to the surface. So, let's take a moment to pause, reflect, and give thanks. You have *The Seed of Hope* and the abounding life within which to cultivate it.

And *that* is a remarkable gift.

YOU
ARE
HERE

Here are a few questions to consider as you germinate your dream. If you cannot answer yes to each of them, see if you can dream even bigger, or find a different plot of soil in which to do so.

Does this dream line up with my core values?

Will fulfilling this dream bring me joy and help my heart dance along the way?

Am I excited to learn the ways this dream will require me to grow and transform? And a little nervous, too?

Will I need help from The Great Mystery for the dream to become a reality? Do I have a picture in my mind that will help me call out for that help?

Will this dream also benefit others? Am I close enough to them to learn how, and why?

Does this dream honor and respect the Earth and the environment?

Following your dream is just like following a north star—you're not heading on a straight line from here to there, you're using that faraway point as a reference. The point is not to get there but to be guided along your way. The journey itself is the treasure.

OWL YOU NEED IS LOVE

Who looks outside, dreams; who looks inside, awakens.
—Carl Jung

Out of the darkness of dreaming into the dawning of day opened two huge, round eyes staring out into endless space. One was the Sun and the other the Moon, and they were known by the stars as the *Two Witnesses*. They worked in tandem, a perfect marriage of opposites. They trusted each other and saw better together. Their vision was aided and enhanced by each other in perception, depth, and focus. But the two eyes were so firmly affixed on *The World* around them that they lost sight of the dream within them. And so a third, all-seeing eye, named Earth, awoke and gazed fiercely between the two others. While the Sun and the Moon looked out, Earth looked inside AND out. Together, these three witnesses became a watchman, a seer and a sage, a wizened protector of dreams and the darkness from which they emerge. These are the eyes of *Sova, the Owl of Observation* and *Keeper of the Color Indigo*.

Perched upon awareness itself, Sova watched over three worlds simultaneously: the worlds of What Was, What Is, and What Could Be. With a gaze that pierced the thickest veils of illusion, she stared straight through *The Gray Area*. She saw its beginning and its demise, and therefore her feathers were not ruffled. Sova sat in stillness, ever aware of *The Great Mystery* and ever alert to what it asked of her.

Sova will help you keep an eye on things. She encourages you to see both sides of every story and the wisdom within each of its pages. She will be a beginner's guide to your beginner's mind. She has looked long before, she is looking right now, and she has vowed to always look after **You**.

I AM MY COLOR'S KEEPER

NAME: SOVA (SO-VAH)
ANIMAL TOTEM: OWL OF OBSERVATION
KEEPER OF THE COLOR: INDIGO
VIRTUE: SEEING OBJECTIVELY
AFFIRMATION: I KNOW WHO I AM
KEEPSAKE: LOOKING GLASSES

You know hoo is watching. Be sure to color in Sova and follow her wise words so you can finally see the light.

In a dark time, the eye begins to see.
—Cavett Robert

SOVA

SIGHT. UNSEEN.

If the doors of perception were cleansed, everything would appear to man as it is: infinite.
—William Blake

BLIND SIDED

There is an Eastern parable of a group of blind men who each touch a different part of an elephant to learn what it is like. The blind man who feels the leg claims that the elephant is like a column or pillar so strong that it could hold up the sky; the man who feels the tail asserts that the elephant is like a rope, twisted and frayed; the one who sits before the elephant and feels its hanging trunk maintains that the elephant is like a tree branch, swooping and supple; the man who touches the elephant's ear professes that the elephant is like a paper fan or a finely woven textile that can be blown in the wind; and the one who feels the tusk contends that the creature is like a spear, sharp and savage.

The blind men share what they have "seen" and realize they all are in complete disagreement. A wise king explains to them that they are each correct from their respective viewpoint. As we allow ourselves to see through the eyes of others, our view of *The World* can widen and expand, and so, too, our compassion. Have fun coloring in all the parts of the elephant, and notice what you see anew.

Where have you been blinded by your beliefs?

....
....
....

Who or what have you come to see in a new light?

....
....
....

The real voyage of discovery consists not in seeking new landscapes but in having new eyes.
—Marcel Proust

THE LIVING LIBRARY

Honesty is the first chapter in the book of wisdom.
—Thomas Jefferson

SHELF LIFE

In *The Living Library*, the shelves are filled with wisdom garnered from the heart. A life well lived will inevitably encounter art and science, fact and fiction, romance and drama, and life lessons can come in the form of the people we meet. On the next page, read the book titles and fill in the name of someone from your life who has authored the equivalent lesson for you.

◆ WITHIN-QUIRIES: ◆

 If your life were composed of five chapters, what would they be?

1. ....
2. ....
3. ....
4. ....
5. ....

 Write out your three biggest life lessons in a quotable form.

1. " .... "
2. " .... "
3. " .... "

The only true wisdom is in knowing you know nothing.
—Socrates

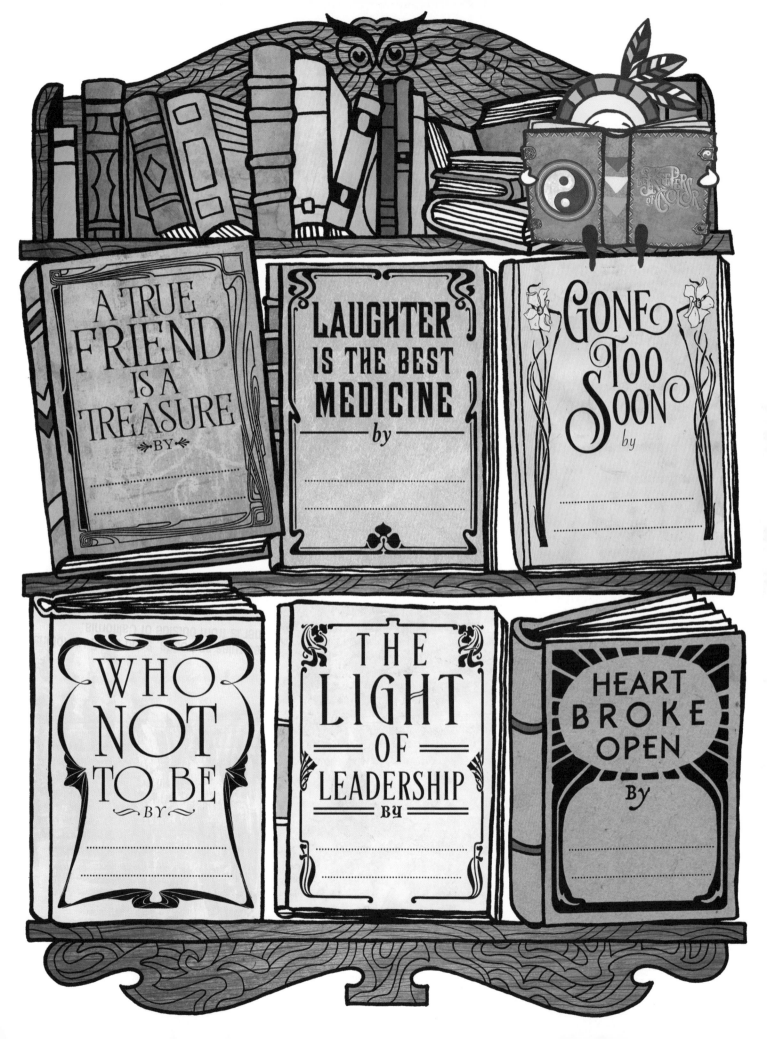

OUT OF SIGHT

All fires begin with a spark. The creative fire that set Life ablaze was no different. In modern days, this primal ignition has been called the "big bang," but this cosmic kindling was neither big nor a bang. It was not a violent or chaotic eruption but a sweet and serene awakening. Yes, the "big bang" was much more like a "blessed blink." And if the eyes are indeed the windows to the soul, then *The Great Mystery* also has eyes, and they, too, were once opened for the very first time. This grand awakening from sleep to sight caused the slightest of frictions, igniting a primordial spark. This was the first twinkle in anyone's eyes— eyes that would soon see everything.

These "eyes" were not made of flesh nor found in any anatomy book. They were, in fact, a way of seeing. Those who gazed through these infinite frames, known as *The Looking Glasses*, could see *The World* in vivid, technicolor clarity: one lens a microscope, the other a telescope; one eye closed, and the other ever open. *The Looking Glasses* are the vision of Visionaries, the sight of all Seers, and the eyes of the blind.

These are the lenses through which *The Great Mystery* gazes upon itself. A literal sight to behold, they have seen every season turn and every forest burn, every *Seed of Hope* come to sprout, every faith and every doubt, every ebb and every flow, the perception of fast and the notion of slow. They have witnessed words from the left and thoughts from the right, praying for peace while watching a fight.

If *The Looking Glasses* have come into your focus, you have learned to listen through the noise and are now being asked to see in the dark. Seeing IS believing, so dust off the filter of other people's perspectives and take a clear-eyed view of *The World Within* you. What situation can you look at from a different point of view? How can you observe someone or something with new eyes? Life is a spectacular spectacle. While our days may be numbered, our gaze is truly limitless. See for yourself!

THE LOOKING GLASSES

THE COURAGE OF COLOR

Victory is within me, and within me I shall go.
—Matthew Love

When the call to adventure is ignored, delayed, or denied—if it has been swallowed up by the muted madness or the drone of dissonance—a special sound is needed. Not the sound of silence or whispers nor the sound of suggestion or counsel but sound, the alarm—a rippling resonance that sets things into place, that forces shudderers to think, and that jogs anyone's memory within earshot of their own hushed heartbeat.

Leo, the Lion of Leadership and *Keeper of the Color Orange*, was born within the bellowing echoes of one such roar. As outer wars continued to be waged and violence and anger continued to be raged, a fever pitch was reached. The winds of change rode in from the East upon a golden chariot and let out a battle cry that shook the very faith and foundation of the heavens.

Out of these reverberations Leo first unfurled himself before the world, kneeling in a humble bow. While one knee rested gently upon the fields of peace, his other foot was firmly planted upon the battlefield. Perpetually poised for pounce or for prayer, Leo fixes his warrior eyes with determination to scan the landscapes before him. His heart beats as a victorious drum, and his shimmering sword is raised in defiance against all things threatening *The Seed of Hope*. Leo is here to lead you toward leadership. Bestowing you with both courage and conviction, he will train you in the art of being a peaceful warrior. Victory is inevitable when you are led by the love of your own heart.

I AM MY COLOR'S KEEPER

NAME: LEO
ANIMAL TOTEM: LION OF LEADERSHIP
KEEPER OF THE COLOR: ORANGE
VIRTUE: DIVINE DUTY
AFFIRMATION: I AM TRIUMPHANT
KEEPSAKE: SWORD

Let's call this a knight! Arm yourself with your most courageous of colors and bravely bring Leo to life. Follow his lead—*The Gray Area* is no match for the lionhearted!

Greater in battle than the man who would conquer a thousand times a thousand men is he who would conquer just one—himself.
—Buddha

LEO

THE LION'S ROAR

Only a lion can recognize a lion's roar.
—Kodo Sawaki

LOUD & PROUD

Leo is here to help you pick your battles. He reminds you that the ultimate victory often lies in a win-win solution where violence is not needed and peace and equanimity reign supreme. There is such power in vulnerability. Speaking your truth and standing up for what you believe takes much courage. We do not need to fight aggression with aggression or fire with fire. To choose happiness over hatred, compassion over competition, and generosity over greed is a tremendous act of bravery. You are mighty. Remember the enormous inner strength and invincible power within you called the love of your own heart.

On the next page, color in the Lion's fiery mane, and as you do so, ask yourself: What are you wanting to say, sing, or roar from your heart? Think about your dream, and in the Lion's mouth, write a declaration you are making so Leo may roar it for *The World* to hear.
Examples: I am_____.
I will_____.

**I am Color.
Hear me roar.**

List three times you have been brave.

What battle are you exhausted from fighting?

Three things cannot be long hidden: the sun, the moon, and the truth.
—Buddha

INNER BATTLE

*When you resort to violence to prove a point,
you've just experienced a profound failure of imagination.*
—Sherman Alexie

Sometimes in life we can feel as if we are under constant attack, from the critics in our heads to the solicitations of society. Even in the midst of chaos there is still space available for you to grow. No matter the circumstances or how thick *The Gray Area* becomes, there is *always* a plot of land waiting for you to claim it and water your dream. Consider that the most courageous act, and the most important thing we can fight for, is to nourish and tend to *The World Within* us. Using your coloring tool, draw some water showering upon the sprout to help your garden (and your courage) grow.

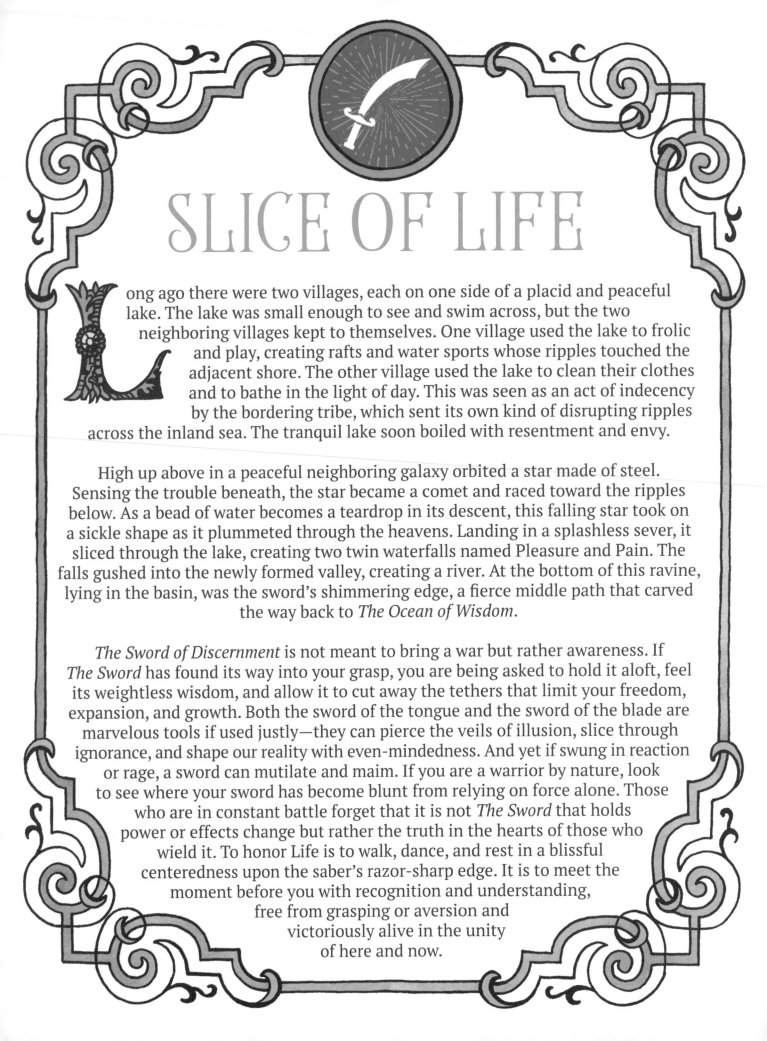

SLICE OF LIFE

Long ago there were two villages, each on one side of a placid and peaceful lake. The lake was small enough to see and swim across, but the two neighboring villages kept to themselves. One village used the lake to frolic and play, creating rafts and water sports whose ripples touched the adjacent shore. The other village used the lake to clean their clothes and to bathe in the light of day. This was seen as an act of indecency by the bordering tribe, which sent its own kind of disrupting ripples across the inland sea. The tranquil lake soon boiled with resentment and envy.

High up above in a peaceful neighboring galaxy orbited a star made of steel. Sensing the trouble beneath, the star became a comet and raced toward the ripples below. As a bead of water becomes a teardrop in its descent, this falling star took on a sickle shape as it plummeted through the heavens. Landing in a splashless sever, it sliced through the lake, creating two twin waterfalls named Pleasure and Pain. The falls gushed into the newly formed valley, creating a river. At the bottom of this ravine, lying in the basin, was the sword's shimmering edge, a fierce middle path that carved the way back to *The Ocean of Wisdom*.

The Sword of Discernment is not meant to bring a war but rather awareness. If *The Sword* has found its way into your grasp, you are being asked to hold it aloft, feel its weightless wisdom, and allow it to cut away the tethers that limit your freedom, expansion, and growth. Both the sword of the tongue and the sword of the blade are marvelous tools if used justly—they can pierce the veils of illusion, slice through ignorance, and shape our reality with even-mindedness. And yet if swung in reaction or rage, a sword can mutilate and maim. If you are a warrior by nature, look to see where your sword has become blunt from relying on force alone. Those who are in constant battle forget that it is not *The Sword* that holds power or effects change but rather the truth in the hearts of those who wield it. To honor Life is to walk, dance, and rest in a blissful centeredness upon the saber's razor-sharp edge. It is to meet the moment before you with recognition and understanding, free from grasping or aversion and victoriously alive in the unity of here and now.

THE SWORD OF DISCERNMENT

Sometimes we have to see it to believe it.
Other times we just have to wait . . .
inside our beliefs . . . and see.
When we begin to see eye to eye and heart to heart,
we view *The World* as it truly is.

Here is where creatures large and small dance together,
where seeds are sown, harvests are reaped, dreams matter, and
the love runs deep—a world where everyone is included in this
glorious game and has more than enough to live and give.

This is a *big* vision,
but not too big to live into.

Let's not take our eyes off the prize
or our mind off being kind!

YOU ARE HERE

YOU ARE AMAZING STAYFOCUSED

It takes incredible courage to bring forth what is within us in the face of doubt and adversity.

We **can** choose to live in ways that build that courage. We **can** pick our battles. We **can** be calm amid the chaos.

There's no better way to sharpen your proverbial sword than to remember your roar as you bravely engage with *The World.*

We've got a few more heroes to meet; let's greet them with a bow of respect and a nod of knowing.

AN EMERGE AND SEE

One is never afraid of the unknown; one is afraid of the known coming to an end.
—Jiddu Krishnamurti

"ME"TAMORPHOSIS

To create a new context for our life is to create a new world of possibility. It requires some major change, and there's probably no greater symbol of change than a butterfly. As soon as a caterpillar is born, it starts eating—usually beginning with the leaf it was born upon. It eats and eats and eats. Consumption is its lifestyle, until one day it's too bloated to even take another bite. So it finds a sturdy perch to hang from and forms a chrysalis. The chrysalis is a womb, an intentional retreat where the caterpillar can focus on the big work it came here to do. This is where the magic happens. Only in the safe swaddle of this cocooning process do new cells within the caterpillar appear. Scientists call them "imaginal cells." You can think of them as visionaries. They hold within them the seemingly absurd idea that a plump, overweight caterpillar can miraculously turn into a totally new creature that knows how to fly. When they first appear, the imaginal cells are so revolutionary in frequency that the caterpillar's immune system starts attacking them, thinking they are foreign enemies. But the imaginal cells hold true to their vision and conviction. They're so faithful to the possibility within them that, one by one and cluster by cluster, the caterpillar's cells join in on the butterfly revolution. Inside the chrysalis, all the cells dissolve into a living liquid, an organic goo that becomes both the builder and the building blocks working in unison to give birth to a beautiful new world.

Look within and see where you're inspired. Consider that this is your own imaginal cell waiting to transform life as you know it. On the following page, follow the imaginal cell's lead by coloring in and activating all the other cells. What do you now see as possible?

Who have you been?

Who are you becoming?

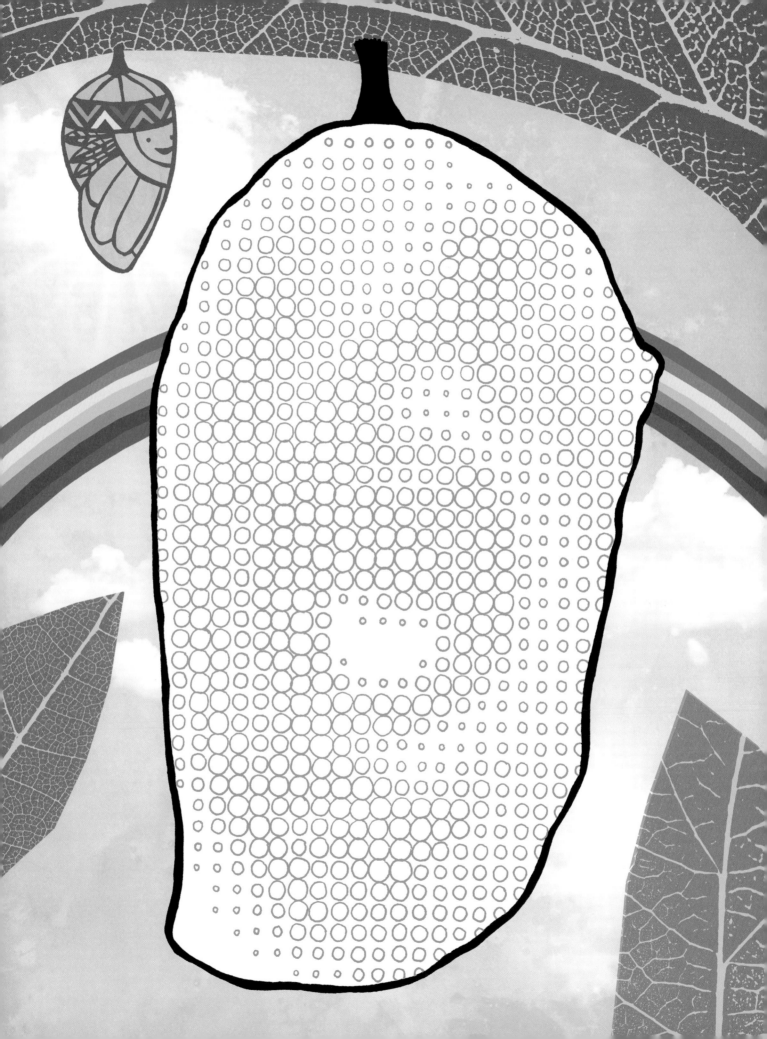

THE BEST OF BOTH WORLDS

What the caterpillar calls the end of the world the master calls a butterfly.
—Richard Bach

Nothing in Nature comes to Life without a seed. Every birth or beginning starts with some sort of inspiration. Imagine a cell—an imaginal cell, an activist, an evolutionary, a cell unafraid to die and unshakably called to live. This one brave cell had a vision, a wild and remarkable vision—a belief that it could better *The World*. The cell caught a glimpse of possibility, and in a flash, it understood what it needed to do.

Change.

Wrapped in the bosom of her own becoming, this cell lit herself from the inside out. She burned with a tenacious hunger and a profound passion. Her mission was spellbinding—an idea so big that *The World as We Know It* could not hold it, though she was not asking it to. She was creating a new world. She was asking it to die the same way the sprout demands *The Seed* to relent, the same way the egg must collapse, the water must break, and Life must live.

And through the intensity of her intention, *Vajra, the Butterfly of Becoming*, became. Breaking out of *The Chrysalis of Creativity*, Vajra's metamorphosis brought the gifts of color and self-expression. The wind of her wings carried compassion and transcendence. Her lightness of being was a messenger of moments and a teacher of transitions. She had heeded Life's call and became what it had beckoned. Vajra has lived *The Great Mystery* and has returned to tell her story to and through You.

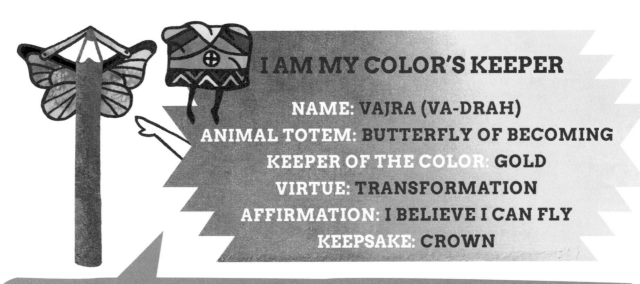

I AM MY COLOR'S KEEPER

NAME: VAJRA (VA-DRAH)
ANIMAL TOTEM: BUTTERFLY OF BECOMING
KEEPER OF THE COLOR: GOLD
VIRTUE: TRANSFORMATION
AFFIRMATION: I BELIEVE I CAN FLY
KEEPSAKE: CROWN

It's time for a change! Let's put on our wings, be a social butterfly, and pass Vajra's exercises with flying colors!

If you begin to understand what you are without trying to change it, then what you are undergoes a transformation.
—Jiddu Krishnamurti

VAJRA

A WING. AND A PRAYER.

Every man takes the limits of his own field of vision for the limits of the world.
—Arthur Schopenhauer

DREAMCATCHER EXERCISE: HERE & BACK AGAIN

Take a moment now, or as you color in the butterflies on the next page, to picture yourself lying in a beautiful meadow. Birds are chirping, the sun is shining, and nature is all around you. Slowly and effortlessly you start floating up in the air and over the flowers. You pass the treetops, feeling light as the breeze as you move toward the clouds. You are being lifted by a loving and graceful presence. As you exit Earth's atmosphere and rise into space, peacefully soaring through the Solar System, you intuitively learn about each planet and their relationship to all things. You continue to drift out beyond this galaxy and past countless others to the farthest reaches of the cosmos—slipping through the starry veils into the realms of muses, angels, and beings of light. You are completely free from your body and even the weight of your soul. Only your consciousness remains. In this state of bliss and cosmic connection, you—the spark, the light, the essence—are given a task, a divine errand, a unique chore that only your spirit can fulfill. Once you receive this transmission, you gracefully start returning back through the layers of light, into the vast ocean of stars, and across the galaxy, bowing to Pluto, Saturn, and Jupiter. You start to approach a bright-blue sapphire orb known as Earth and descend into its world. You see the continents below, the oceans, waterways, glaciers, and forests. You see cities and towns bustling with commerce and nations protecting their invisible boundaries. You see poverty and plentitude, hunger and hopefulness, suffering and serenity. You come fully back into your body, and as you land gently atop the Earth like a butterfly upon a flower, you answer the question below.

What did you come here to do?

....
....
....
....
....
....

We shall not cease from exploration, and the end of all our exploring will be to arrive where we started and know the place for the first time.
—T. S. Eliot

KINGDOM COME

There once was a king and a queen who lived as husband and wife and were unaware of their royal heritage. They wore neither power nor prestige. In fact, they wore nearly nothing at all, walking barefoot as farmers, at one with the Earth. The couple trusted that *The Great Mystery* would provide for them as it always so lovingly had. Each season they planted the same seeds, and every season in turn they reaped the same harvest. It was always just enough for the two of them. They were grateful for their simple lives and needed nothing more.

But one year hardship struck. The weather changed drastically, and summer never departed. The searing heat beat down on the land, parching the soil. The husband and wife knew there would be no harvest to come. Secretly they each clutched a *Seed of Hope*, too fearful to plant them, wishing the corn, rye, or heirloom fruits would somehow sprout. But they did not, and the holy land became dusty and dry, cracking open in the rainless and sizzling sun. As they kneeled together on the barren ground, they prayed for a sign for how to proceed. And then, floating like a mirage in the middle of the sun-scorched fields, appeared a crown. The golden crown, glowing like a field of wheat, spoke a mighty and merciful message: "Plant your *Seed* and share your harvest." The farmers took heed, the lands were restored, and abundance abounded.

Invisible to the eye and blinding to the soul, *The Crown of Compassion* cannot be seen but is undeniably felt. It is not worn on heads but rather on hearts—brave and courageous hearts that are willing to follow the peaceful guidance of inner governance. *The Crown* recognizes and bows to the nobility in all beings. It sees Hope and Transformation in every soul. And when *The Crown* is worn, kingdoms of kindness open their gates before you.

These *Crowns* seek stewards of the Earth—those whose feet walk upon this world and whose thrones sit regally upon another. *The Crown* summons them to stand up and stand together in solidarity. It is a royal reminder of your place within *The Great Mystery* as you preside and govern over *The World Within*.
Yes, you're majesty.

THE CROWN OF COMPASSION

PROTECT THE SACRED

Looking behind, I am filled with gratitude; looking forward, I am filled with vision; looking upward, I am filled with strength; looking within, I discover peace.
—Quero Apache prayer

Out of darkness came the light, and out of the light was birthed a bright white bison, *Oyate*, a legendary Peacemaker, an Earth Elder, and *Keeper of the Color White*. Oyate is the son of the Sun. He rises each morning, pure as the driven snow, as grandfather and grandchild, wise and wondrous, student and sage. He is a daylight star that burns like a bonfire in the clear blue sky.

No color shines brighter than White, for it is where all colors commune and is the hue that calls each of them home. Wizened by the wisdom within White, the secrets sealed in the spectrum, and the promise protected by the prism, Oyate was a *Keeper* of both *Color* and consciousness.

Oyate went to work on behalf of *The Seed*'s seeds. He oversaw *The Orchard of Opportunity* and looked after future generations, teaching them to become abundantly alive and to share their gifts with *The World*. He was a leader of leaders, a king of kings, and ruler of *The Rainbow*. He was as upright, noble, kindhearted, and brave as you'd want a loving leader to be, a loud and proud gentle giant who governs with grace as he romps and roams.

Life is his church, the sky is his shelter, silence his spokesperson, love his answer, wisdom his waters, fire his friend. Now is his gift. You are his equal.

I AM MY COLOR'S KEEPER

NAME: OYATE (OY-YA-TAY)
ANIMAL TOTEM: BISON OF BENEDICTION
KEEPER OF THE COLOR: WHITE
VIRTUE: PROTECTING THE SACRED
AFFIRMATION:
MAY ALL BEINGS BE AT PEACE
KEEPSAKE: DREAMCATCHER

The love, light, and magical bison within me honors the love, light, and magical bison within you.

The Holy Land is everywhere.
—Black Elk

OYATE

THE PRAYER WE BREATHE

For although He is right with us and in and out of us and all through us,
we have to go on journeys to find Him.
—Thomas Merton

BLOWIN' IN THE WIND

You've made quite a journey through this book.
Take a breath for a moment and look back over your life.
On the flags on the next page, write your prayers for
yourself and your prayers for *The World*. Carry them with
you from here on out, and use your life to see that these
words come true. The wind is in your favor!

❖ WITHIN-QUIRIES: ❖

What metaphorical mountains have you climbed?

Name five unique blessings in your life.

1.
2.
3.
4.
5.

Happiness is not about making it to the peak of the mountain, nor is it about climbing aimlessly
around the mountain; happiness is the experience of climbing toward the peak.
—Tal Ben-Shahar

THE GREAT DIVIDE

Abandon all your supports. Cast off your dependency on everything external and rely on the Self alone.
—Bhagavad Gita

DRAW. BRIDGE.

You have made it this far, and the training wheels are coming off. Leave your past here and step confidently toward the life calling to you. Even if your legs are shaking, take the next step. Pray. Listen to your intuition. Ask for help. Look for signs.

On the next page, draw a bridge from one side of the divide to the other. Your life is the path before you. When following the call to adventure, we learn to walk this way—step by courageous step, with faith in yourself, what's right in front of you, and in *The Great Mystery.*

❖ WITHIN-QUIRIES: ❖

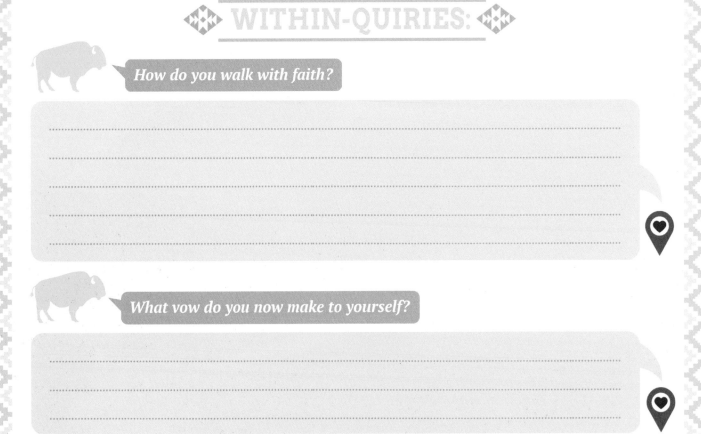

How do you walk with faith?

What vow do you now make to yourself?

The mind creates the abyss; the heart crosses it.
—Nisargadatta Maharaj

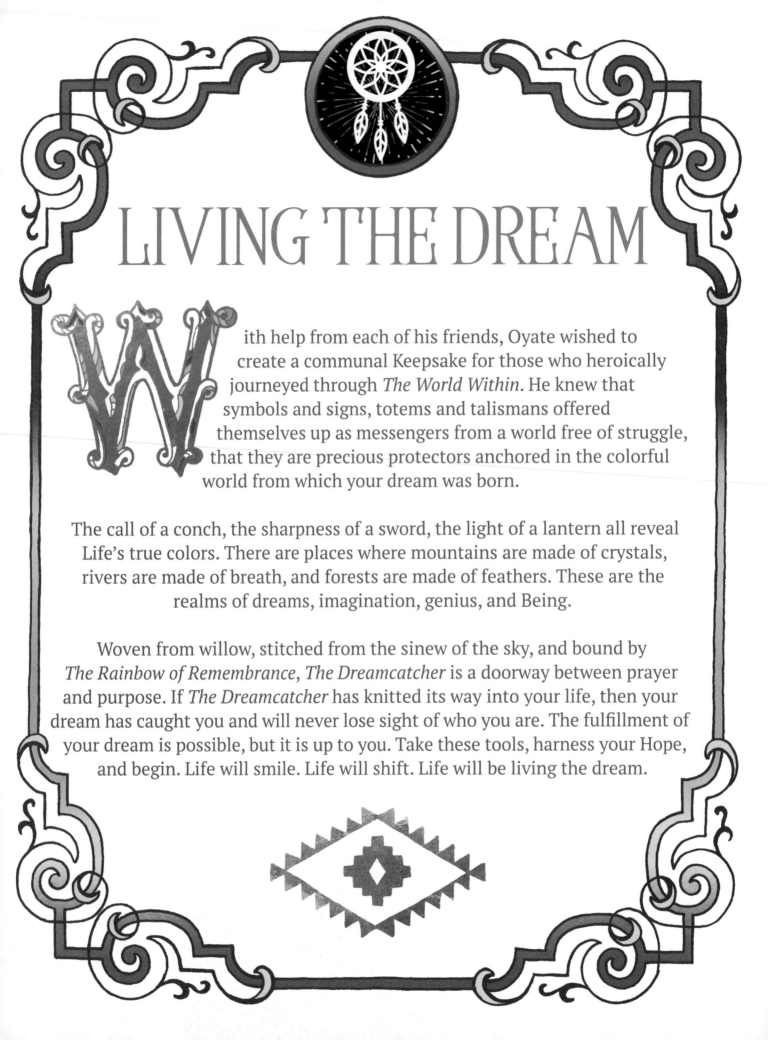

LIVING THE DREAM

With help from each of his friends, Oyate wished to create a communal Keepsake for those who heroically journeyed through *The World Within*. He knew that symbols and signs, totems and talismans offered themselves up as messengers from a world free of struggle, that they are precious protectors anchored in the colorful world from which your dream was born.

The call of a conch, the sharpness of a sword, the light of a lantern all reveal Life's true colors. There are places where mountains are made of crystals, rivers are made of breath, and forests are made of feathers. These are the realms of dreams, imagination, genius, and Being.

Woven from willow, stitched from the sinew of the sky, and bound by *The Rainbow of Remembrance*, *The Dreamcatcher* is a doorway between prayer and purpose. If *The Dreamcatcher* has knitted its way into your life, then your dream has caught you and will never lose sight of who you are. The fulfillment of your dream is possible, but it is up to you. Take these tools, harness your Hope, and begin. Life will smile. Life will shift. Life will be living the dream.

THE DREAMCATCHER

And we're back! What a journey! You are here—right where you need to be.

Welcome here; welcome home. Isn't it funny that your life getting turned upside down is also coming full circle? The end was already there at the beginning.

As with any journey, there is change and a place that stays solid and unchanged. *It's like a crown you forgot you were wearing.*

Walk with it. Talk with it. Be in *The World* wearing your invisible crown. Listen to *The Seed*. It will provide the adventure—you simply get to say **YES**.
Again and many times again.

There is no dream *The Dreamcatcher* cannot hold.

I leave you with a deep bow of respect, a grateful heart, and my trusty golden pencil. This book is just a chapter; you get to create the rest of your story.

Write it, draw it, sing it, dance it, dream it! Let it blossom in all the hearts around you, and in *The World as We Know It.*
Live your story.
I hope it will have even more Color than you could ever imagine.
One last thing: I know we went on this journey to find your dream . . .
but I'm so glad I found YOU.

THE TREE OF TRANSFORMATION

Keep some room in your heart for the unimaginable.
—Mary Oliver

DEEP ROOTS

The Seed is Life's gift to you, and *The Tree* is your gift back to Life. A tree needs time, it needs space, and it needs freedom to stretch its branches and weave its roots in all sorts of directions until it stands in one place. *The Tree of Transformation* grows from *The Seed of Hope*. It takes root in *The World Within* and blooms beautifully to life in *The World as We Know It*.

The Tree is symbolic of your dream realized. On the next page, you are going to draw your *Tree of Transformation*. As you draw your *Tree*, feel what it's like to birth something from the inside out. *The Seed* can no longer contain what wants to come through you. *The Tree* has risen through the rich and fertile darkness, and its branches are now outstretched in the light of day. It's rooted firmly, whole and complete and knowing who it is and what fruits it offers to *The World*. Draw your experience coming to Life.

The Tree is a sign that balance has been restored to the Kingdom. In the space below or on a separate piece of paper, write a love letter to Life, to your kingdom. This could be a song, a poem, a prayer, a myth, or a mantra that salutes and sings the praises of either of *The Worlds*. Write the laws and loves of your land. Call out to *The Keepers*, sing from the treetops, and let Life know you have returned.

Ours is not the task of fixing the entire world at once, but of stretching out to mend the part of the world that is within our reach.
—Clarissa Pinkola Estés

Legend tells of a change that changed everything. Some thought this to be *The End of All Endings*, a fiery or frozen disaster that was self-made or self-deserved and that would bring the demise of *The World as We Know It*. But in times of great crisis, a tension of tensions arises, a mythic pressure of strain and suspense. For those who can balance between uncertainty and excitement—without giving preference or prejudice to either—a new way, unexpected and unseen, springs forth. This middle way, born of grace and surrender, allows Hope to become visible and Life to become viable.

The Keepers knew that when all seemed lost, when *The World* appeared on the brink of collapse and at the edge of some great abyss—this was when and where heroes and heroines emerged. When Hope, Beauty, Inspiration, and Love have been snatched away by the jaws of Doubt, nothing less than wholeheartedness and total conviction would suffice. This was their call.

And their call persisted.

It got deeper, brighter, and more resonant as responses began to appear. Chins began to rise, spines straightened, and feet defiantly danced. A new tale was being told.

Kōan had chased his own tail all the way to a new tale. His painfully elaborate searching had been satiated by the sweetest of simplicities. He shed his skin. She felt renewed in the realization that there was no such thing as enlightened retirement, that there is no END—Life is alive, *The Mystery* is endless, and so, too, is the fire in his heart. Answers were not the answer, but her questions were. Realizing this, a well-fed Kōan slid contently into place, restoring balance to Yin and Yang.

A silent and spirited groundswell emerged. One by one, beings began to heed the call within themselves. Instead of pointing fingers, they got down to work. They took full responsibility for their lives and tended to their own *Gray Areas*. They knew that something precious had been lost and could be found only where others feared to go. So they faced their fears, saluted their shadows, and dealt with their doubts. *The World Within* became a destination, not a detour.

These individuals took Life into their own hands—not with any form of violence or struggle but with the slightest of shifts inward. They began to believe in themselves, in their innate nobility, in living creativity, in the power of Love, and in the commitment to compassion. They each realized and reawakened to who they were—worthy, confident, and capable—and they began to live these truths. They each became a *Keeper of Color*.

A *Keeper of Color* is also a *Keeper* of one's Word and one's Wonder, a *Keeper* of Prayer and Promise, Creativity and Consciousness, Earth and Earnesty.

A *Keeper* fights not with another but only to bring out the best in themselves. A *Keeper* does not protect *The Great Mystery* but rather lives within it—and *The Great Mystery* protects them. A *Keeper* does not set out to save the whole world; they bring forth what is within them, and the wholeness of *The World* is saved.

These newly appointed *Keepers* planted their *Seeds of Hope* straight into the heart of these darkened times. Color reemerged, inspiration blossomed, and awakening awoke. Life became a perennial spring, a vibrant and ceaseless season that honored *The World Within* each and every being.

Life's true calling is to LIVE. Life always finds a way. It finds a million tiny, wondrous, miraculous ways. Like a seed growing through concrete—Life finds a way. Like the rains after a drought—Life finds a way. Like you reading this book right now—Life finds a way . . .

The World did not end, nor did this book.
It became *The Seed* of a billion new beginnings.
But not before it all came undone.

Life was then put back better than we had found it, wondrous and alive. Dreams were restored, and with them the knowingness that they can come true. Seekers sought, and *The Keepers* kept their eyes and ears toward transformation. A new *World* emerged. Each dreamer became an imaginal cell in a planetwide personal metamorphosis. All those who said yes to their calling awoke to the delight of *The Great Mystery*, and *The Rainbow of Remembrance* came full circle, reminding itself and all others just why:

YOU
ARE
HERE